Central Europe

MANAGING EDITORS
Amy Bauman
Barbara J. Behm

CONTENT EDITORS
Amanda Barrickman
James I. Clark
Patricia Lantier
Charles P. Milne, Jr.
Katherine C. Noonan
Christine Snyder
Gary Turbak
William M. Vogt
Denise A. Wenger
Harold L. Willis
John Wolf

ASSISTANT EDITORS
Ann Angel
Michelle Dambeck
Barbara Murray
Renee Prink
Andrea J. Schneider

INDEXER
James I. Clark

ART/PRODUCTION
Suzanne Beck, Art Director
Andrew Rupniewski, Production Manager
Eileen Rickey, Typesetter

Library of Congress Number: 88-18337

2 3 4 5 6 7 8 9 0   97 96 95 94 93 92

Library of Congress Cataloging-in-Publication Data

Bottoni, Luciana.
  [Europa centrale, English]
  Central Europe / Luciana Bottoni.
  — (World nature encyclopedia)
  Translation of: Europa centrale.
  Includes index.
  Summary: Describes the plant and animal life of Central
Europe and its interaction with the environment.
  1. Ecology—Central Europe—Juvenile literature.
[1. Ecology—Central Europe. 2. Central Europe.]
I. Bottoni, Luciana, 1952-. II. Title. III. Series: Natura nel
mondo. English.
QH135.E913 1988 574.5′.264′0943—dc19   88-18386
ISBN 0-8172-3325-3

WORLD NATURE ENCYCLOPEDIA

Central Europe

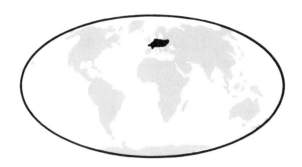

Luciana Bottoni
Valeria Lucini
Renato Massa
Vittorio Vigorita

RAINTREE
STECK-VAUGHN
L I B R A R Y

Austin, Texas

CONTENTS

INTRODUCTION

Seen from an airplane, most of central Europe appears as a large plain made up of many little squares and rectangles of different colors. These are cultivated farmlands. Through the centuries, they have replaced almost every type of natural environment. This was not always so. In the past, central Europe was dominated by forests of leafy trees. They had large populations of many different types of animals living in them. Also, near the rivers and lakes there were large marshes that were abundant with wildlife. In these areas, storks, pelicans, herons, geese, beavers, wild boar, and many other animals could be found.

The plains of central Europe from France to Russia were covered with forests, marshes, and steppes (grass-covered plains with scattered trees). Even today, among the highways, cities, factories, and thousands of other traces of human activities, you can still find some forests, marshes, and steppes. Of course, the intense activities of humans have greatly changed the original environments. Many marshes and forests have been either eliminated or greatly reduced in size. The steppe has been changed into a so-called cultivated steppe. Here most of the plants are grain crops used for feeding people.

The result of this environmental change was a large reduction in the populations of animals that inhabited (and still inhabit) the heart of the European continent. Similar changes which occurred in North America were more sudden and very violent, but in central Europe, each change occurred gradually. No species of animal became extinct. However, many animals, especially the larger ones that lived in forests and marshes, became restricted to small refuge areas. They had to adapt to a world that was dominated by humans, not other animals.

At first, many of the animal species that lived on the steppe greatly benefited from this new situation. They spread into new areas, and their numbers grew much larger. However, in the last decades, even this cultivated steppe created by humans has undergone a dramatic new change. The agricultural methods have become more and more intensified. The hedges between fields have often been cut down.

This book will discuss the cultivated steppe, the forests and marshes of central Europe, and the plants and animals of these environments. Although they can exist in only tiny patches of territory, they are still alive and vital.

FROM PAST TO PRESENT

If modern travelers could use a time machine, they would be truly amazed to tour the Europe of the past. There would not be boring flat fields of cultivated grain alternating with "jungles" of asphalt and cement. Instead, they would see hundreds of miles of unspoiled forests and large rivers and marshes. These reached from the Atlantic coasts across the large central plains to the Ural Mountain chain in the Soviet Union. The astonished tourist would probably decide that the dramatic change of this landscape was caused by the modern technologies of the twentieth century. Actually, the destruction and transformation of these natural environments began in the stone age, although it was not as rapid then as in recent times.

Deforestation and Reforestation

In the Neolithic age ("new stone age") of ten thousand years ago, people began to clear the forests with axes and fire. They did this without seriously damaging or changing the environment. This is because the population of humans was small and their tools were rather simple and limited. It was only around 1000 B.C. that the forests became an obstacle to human activities. At that time, humans gradually stopped eating wild animals, roots, seeds, and fruits and began cultivating the land.

Since then, the work of deforestation happened rapidly. It can be said that the growth of human civilization happened at the same speed as the deforestation. For example, during the Middle Ages (476 to 1500 A.D.), people believed strongly that the forests should be destroyed.

The disorganized deforestation in Europe was finally stopped in the twentieth century. Since the beginning of this century, the total area of forested land has stopped shrinking. In several countries, the amount of wooded land is actually increasing due to reforestation (the planting of trees). Today however, much of the forested land is "cultivated," meaning that people determine the location, height, life span, and species of trees. The types of trees that are grown are carefully selected according to the needs of people, so the original tree species of the European forests have been almost completely replaced by species from other areas or even from other continents.

The Original Forests

History does not give clear information on the composition of the ancient forest. More exact information can be

Preceding pages: Homes, cultivated fields, and forests are seen at Bad Schwalbach in the Renania Palatinate (West Germany). Most of central Europe looks like a checkerboard of cities, agricultural areas, and forests.

Opposite page: Shown is a pile of recently-cut logs in a forest of the Alps. Today, forestry and modern farming methods are widely used to better conserve natural resources, even though this changes the original nature of the forests. However, this was not always true. Many forests, especially in the plains and in the hills, were cut down completely to make space for human activities.

obtained from the fossil pollen in many European peat bogs. Peat bogs are marshy areas where plant material collects over many hundreds of years. By looking at this evidence, it is determined that the distribution of the tree species varied in different types of soil and climate.

The most common trees were deciduous (trees that lose their leaves every year). Oaks and other deciduous trees such as beeches, maples, alders, hornbeams, ashes, and basswoods adapted to the severe central European winters. Beech trees dominated areas that had heavy rainfall and soil that contained limestone particles. Their dense foilage or leaves, completely shaded the ground from the sun's rays. This helped the growth of young beech trees.

The marshlands were dominated by alders, which formed "tunnel forests" arching over the waterways. In the moors and in areas that were damaged by fires, there were thin beech forests similar to the forests found at the edge of the tundra. Moors are areas of poorly drained, open land with patches of peat bogs and heath plants.

There is information on the density, and distribution of these forests from sources dating as far back as Julius Caesar, who wrote that the forest north of the Alps was "nine days wide. It begins at the borders of the Alps and follows the course of the Danube River as far as the land of the Thracians [the ancient country of Thrace in the region of

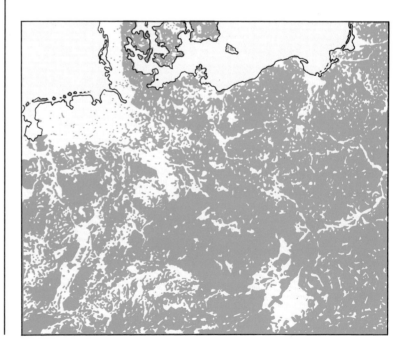

This graph shows the amount of forest in central Europe around the year 900 A.D. A major portion of the continent was still covered by forests with very large animal species living in them.

the modern country of Bulgaria, south of Romania]. From there, turning left from the river, it continues across a multitude of different regions. Although many people of the country [Rome] have traveled for six days into this forest, no one has reported to have reached the end nor to have discovered how far it extends."

The Present Forests

Only small "islands" remain of the vast forests mentioned by Julius Caesar and these are scattered among the open, cultivated plains. Over a period of a thousand years, the destruction of the forest has affected the climate, the bodies of water and the soil. This has resulted in great changes in the entire environment of central Europe. Today, the forests have not only been extremely reduced in area, but they also have become quite mixed in their species composition.

An exception to this mixing of species is found in the forest of Bialowieza, located between Poland and the Soviet Union. This forest covers a total area of 498 square miles (129,000 hectares). The 19-square-mile (5,000 ha) area in Poland is protected as a reserve. The most typical trees here are bay oaks and Norway spruces, which grow well on the plains in this area. The other trees found here are birches, beeches, poplars, ashes, Scotch pines, maples, mountain

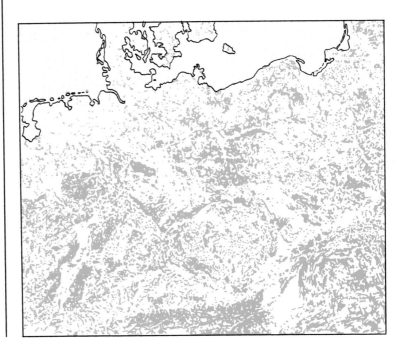

This graph shows the amount of forest in central Europe around the year 1900. The forest area has been greatly reduced and broken up. As a result, the large-sized animals are now only found in national parks and nature reserves.

This view is of the Fontana Forest, which is a few miles from the city of Mantova, Italy. Although it has been greatly changed by the planting of exotic (foreign) tree and herb species, a few areas of original plains forest still remain. This forest is very important from a scientific standpoint. These are the last remaining environments which are ideal for many species of animals and plants that have now completely disappeared from the open areas of the plains.

ashes, junipers, and a few rare larches. This is a northern European version of the central European mixed forest. Some species of plants and animals found here are typical of the conifer forests of the north, the so-called taiga.

The forests of the Po River plains in northern Italy are at the other extreme of central Europe, if climate and change by humans are considered. For example, the 575-acre (233 ha) Fontana Forest near Mantova, Italy, has a unique variety of trees, shrubs, and herbaceous plants (those that are green and leafy, not woody). British oak, white hornbeam, service trees, common maples, and wild cherries dominate the forest.

Tunnel Forests, Poplar Forests, and Moors

Today, only small patches of the European plains forests still survive. These are either surrounded by cultivated fields or they are found as thin strips along rivers and creeks, especially where many people live. These forests are often greatly changed by humans. Two tree species, white poplar and white willow, dominate the vegetation. These are grown like a crop. The herbaceous plants include many species from other continents, such as poke, late goldenrod, Persian speedwell, crabgrass, and horseweed. Often these exotic plants are very conspicuous and spread quickly.

The best example of an exotic species is the locust tree. This tree, from North America, can reach a height of 65 to 82 feet (20 to 25 meters). It is common not only along streams, but just about everywhere. It forms thick bunches of shrubs called "thickets" or even woods that are sometimes mixed with native species. This species quickly invades almost any empty space, such as an old forest with some trees cut out, poplar woods, or cultivated fields which have been neglected.

The locust tends to form mixed forests with native species of trees such as oaks, hazelnuts, birches, and Scotch pines. Scotch pines, which are very common on the plains of Germany, give rise to a certain type of environment called a "moor." In a moor, the wide spaces between the Scotch pines are occupied by a thick undergrowth of heather shrubs with typical, small, pink flowers.

The Spore-producing Plants of the Forest

In the undergrowth of all the humid forests of the world, many plants live which do not reproduce by flowers, but by very small spores. Spores are reproductive cells that pro-

Yellow pholiota mushrooms grow on an old tree trunk. This small fungus usually grows in clusters on decaying wood. It appears from spring to late fall. Mushroom hunters collect this species, since it is a very tasty edible fungus. Along with the meadow mushroom, it has been cultivated successfully. This is done by transplanting the growing threads (mycelium) of the mushroom onto decaying logs.

duce a new plant when the environmental conditions are favorable. These plant species are called *cryptograms*, which in Greek means "hidden marriage." This term indicates the absence of flowers.

These plants include ferns, horsetails, club mosses, mosses, liverworts, and fungi. Fungi, unlike all the other plants of the group, do not have chlorophyll (the green pigment in leaves that uses the sun's energy to produce food). They must obtain nutrients form organic matter, such as decaying leaves or wood. The cells of fungi contain substances that are also found in animals. For these reasons, most biologists classify fungi in a kingdom of their own, distinct from the typical plants and animals.

Unlike algae, the so-called land plants such as ferns, horsetails, club mosses, mosses, and liverworts, have tissues or groups of cells that carry water and nutrients. All of them have two different plant forms, or generations, that alternate with each other. The first plant produces another plant with a different shape and size. The second plant grows for a period of time and then produces a new plant like the first plant (or generation). The two different generations of plants alternate with each other. These generations differ in size and in their number of chromosomes which are gene-carrying parts of the cell.

The second generation of mosses and liverworts is their largest and most commonly seen form. However, with ferns, the first generation is the largest and most commonly seen form. In ferns, which are usually considered to be more evolved, the second generation is a small plant resembling a tiny leaf, the size of a fingernail. This grows on the ground and is easily overlooked by those who are not plant experts.

Wetlands

The vegetation of the central European wetlands is quite unusual. Interesting specimens can be seen by pools of water, lakes, springs arising in flatlands, and oxbows. Oxbows are U-shaped river bends that have been cut off from the flowing river. Other wetland environments include impermeable land which remains wet after a rain, and artificial bodies of water. Examples of artificial wetlands are old rock quarries and fields flooded by springs or canals.

Along the larger bodies of water, the most common vegetation is made up of sedges, reeds, spike-rushes, burr-

A birch woods is seen in the foothills of the Alps. The white birch is typical of cool, sunny environments. It grows over a large area, including central Europe, the Apennine Mountain chain in Italy, the Balkan Mountains, and much of northern Europe. Also in the north is the brown birch. It grows in colder, wetter areas, and on poorer soils that are acidic and peaty (having peat, which is a layer of dead plant material that has not completely decayed).

15

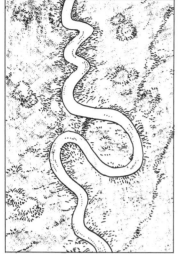

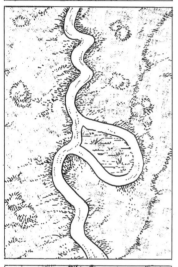

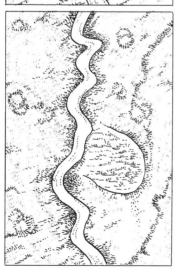

reeds, and reedgrasses. The plants growing underwater include water buttercups, water-milfoils, pondweed, duckweed, elodeas, and sometimes white and yellow water lilies.

In the peat bogs, the main plants are the sphagnum mosses, which absorb enormous amounts of water and gradually form floating "rafts." Over the years, this process completely fills the water with soil and vegetation as silt collects and other plants grow.

The "Cultivated Steppe"

The European environment that corresponds to the great prairies of North America is the steppe. Today, this original environment is found only in a few nature reserves located on the plains of the Ukraine and southern Russia, north of the Black Sea and the Caucasus Mountain region. This environment is dominated by various species of fescue grasses and wormwoods mixed with several legumes and sedges.

Above: The marsh of Kopacki Rit is found in Yugoslavia. The extremely high production of living matter substances by the plant life (as a result of photosynthesis) makes wetland environments interesting for the student of biology. These areas are also valuable to fish farmers or animal raisers. It is possible to raise certain animals in marshes without plowing or seeding and without using chemical fertilizers, herbicides, and pesticides.

Opposite page: The illustration shows the stages of forming an oxbow, which is a wetland area that used to be part of a river. The curving river sometimes develops new, straighter channels. Sometimes permanent lakes form from the oxbows if they are fed by underground water.

After the last glaciation of the Quaternary period before the forests almost completely covered central Europe, the steppe environment was widespread. Following the increase of the forests and the later deforestation by humans, the original steppe was replaced by an artificial environment formed by large areas of cultivated grasses. These grass plants are grains including wheat, barley, corn, hay, and others.

The new environments have been named the "cultivated steppe." Several of the most adaptable animal species that lived in the ancient steppes are now found in the cultivated areas along with the most adaptable animal species of the forest. These last animals are only found in the hedges between fields or the thin strips of woods along streams. The species that required certain definite habitats or food were not successful in adapting to the new conditions. Therefore, these animal species are only found in wild and remote environments.

THE HOOFED ANIMALS OF THE FOREST

Among the large herbivores, or plant-eaters, that inhabited the ancient forests of central Europe were the wisent (European bison) and the aurochs, or wild ox. The aurochs became extinct several centuries ago. The wisent, although no longer found in the wild, was barely saved and survives in zoos throughout the world.

Other hoofed animals, such as the European red deer, roe deer, and wild boar, have withstood the reduction of their natural habitats. They have adapted to living in whatever small strips of habitat that remain. They often enter cultivated fields to feed.

The Aurochs and the Wisents

In his long journey through the endless, deep forests of Germany, Julius Caesar found an enormous, majestic wild ox. This animal was the aurochs. Its size was so large that Caesar compared it to a small elephant. Remains of this enormous hoofed animal have been found throughout Europe, from Spain to England and from France to western Asia and the Near East. Its existence also has been shown by prehistoric cave drawings.

The Swiss naturalist Konrad von Gesner (1516-1565) described in detail the characteristics of the aurochs in his well-known animal history book entitled *Historia Animalium*. He was able to do this by looking at the many drawings and paintings that had been made of this animal through the centuries. Male aurochs, similar to black bulls, were 6 feet (2 m) tall. They had long coats of hair, forward-curving horns and curly hair on the forehead. The females and young had light-colored coats of hair.

During the summer, aurochs grazed in herds in open areas, while in winter they lived by themselves in the forest. Then they ate shrubs and trees. This type of diet was the reason their numbers fell. Between the sixth and the ninth centuries A.D., the populations of this wild ox had been reduced because of the cutting of forests by people. For example, in France its numbers were so low that only the king was allowed to hunt it. By 1500, aurochs were present only in several provinces of Poland. In 1599, a herd of only twenty-four was counted. The last female aurochs died in 1627.

In the last centuries of its existence, the European wild oxen mated with domestic oxen. They produced offspring which kept some of the aurochs' characteristics up to the present time. For example, the domestic oxen of Corsica

Opposite page: Roe deer feed on the leaves of a shrub. This deer is the smallest hoofed animal of the forest. It is also the most adaptable and widespread. It is even found in small villages and cultivated fields. The roe deer often enters gardens, and it is sometimes seen on paved roads. It has adapted well to the conditions of the modern world.

19

The aurochs is the ancestor of domestic cattle. It became extinct at the beginning of the seventeenth century. The aurochs probably evolved from an ancestor that also lived in Asia Minor and North Africa. Evidence for this comes from drawings and paintings of an animal similar to the aurochs from ancient Egyptian and Assyrian sculptures. This animal was also mentioned in the Bible as "Re-em." The last written proof of the aurochs' existence comes from a document written by the Baron of Herbestein during 1513-1533. Under a drawing of the animal he wrote: "I am the aurochs, called Thur by the Poles, Aurox by the Germans, and sometimes even bison by the ignorant."

and Spain have a similar curvature of the horns and hair that is similar in color.

The herbivorous wisent lived alongside the aurochs in the prehistoric period, and it was just as impressive in size. The wisent and the American bison descended from the same ancient ancestor through two different migrations. The fossil remains of this ancient bison have been found in northern India. Both the European and American species of bison evolved into different forms—the European wood bison, known as the wisent, and the bison of the steppe, which was already extinct by the last glaciation.

The wisent is smaller than its American relative, even though it reaches a height of 6 feet (2 m) and a weight of 2,205 pounds (1,000 kilograms). Its horns grow sideways, curving upward at first, then turning in a forward direction before finally turning inward. The wisent has thick, dark brown or black hair. It is rather long on the head and the lower part of the body, especially on the neck, chin, and lower front legs.

A long time ago, the wisent could be found in much of Europe where the weather was mild. It probably could be found as far north as Siberia in Asia. Its gradual disappear-

The last wisents (European bison) living in the wild in the forest of Bialowieza were killed by hungry soldiers during the Russian Revolution and World War I. Luckily, several wisents remained in the various zoos throughout the world. These animals were able to reproduce in captivity. The zoos carefully selected the animals to be mated, avoiding blood relationships that were too close (otherwise the offspring would have been less healthy). As a result of this breeding program, there are now over two thousand wisents in the world. They are found mainly in Poland and the Soviet Union, and they are exported to various countries.

ance was caused by widespread hunting and the increased cutting of large areas of forests. Its diet was mainly twigs, bark, and branches of trees and shrubs, plus acorns, mushrooms, and lichens. There is evidence that it lived in Switzerland up to the eleventh century. Since the nineteenth century, the forest of Bialowieza had been its main refuge. In 1914, a herd of about five hundred wisents was living in this forest between Poland and the Soviet Union. World War I and the Russian Revolution gave the final blow to this remaining population. The last wild wisent was believed to be killed by a poacher in 1921.

Today, the wisent would be only a memory if zoos had not captured several specimens of this animal at Bialowieza at the beginning of this century. The efforts of several zoo directors successfully ensured that this species would survive. They set up a reproduction program for the wisent in captivity. A small herd of wisents was released in the original forest of Bialowieza in 1956. The release of these animals over a period of a few decades has resulted in a large growth of the herd. Now it is possible to study the behavior of this species in the wild.

The European Red Deer, Roe Deer, and Wild Boar

Now that the aurochs is extinct and the wisent is found in very small populations, the red deer is the largest hoofed animal in most areas of forest in central Europe. In the southwestern regions, the red deer reaches a height of 47 to 59 inches (120 to 150 cm) at the shoulder and a weight of 200 to 330 pounds (90 to 150 kg). However, in the northeastern regions, it weighs 660 to 770 pounds (300 to 350 kg). The red deer inhabits both broad-leaved and conifer forests near flat or rolling pasture lands.

Unlike the aurochs and the wisents, which were not able to adapt to gradual deforestation, three other hoofed animals of the deciduous forest were able to successfully adapt to the changing conditions. These are the European red deer, the roe deer, and the wild boar. These species require only a small amount of forest to thrive, even in areas that are highly urbanized.

The distribution of the European red deer indicates

that this animal has a great ability to adapt. In fact, it is found from the moors of Scotland to the Swiss forests and to the wooded steppes of southern Russia. The differences between the numerous red deer are in their body weight and the structure of their antlers. These differences are caused partly by inheritance, but also result from the animals' environment, especially the availability of food. This was shown by an experiment done in 1870. Red deer from a Scottish population which reached a maximum weight of 220 pounds (100 kg), with antlers having fourteen points, were taken to New Zealand. In less than twenty years in this new country, a population of red deer was produced that weighed an average of more than 440 pounds (200 kg) with antlers having more than twenty points.

The impressive branched antlers are certainly the most striking feature of the European red deer. The shedding and regrowth of the antlers each year is related to the social behavior of this species. Toward the end of winter, the large antlers fall off the males. Just a slight bump against a low branch of a tree will knock them off. The antlers begin to grow again in spring. They are fully developed by the end of summer.

The basic difference between horns of bovidae (cattle, sheep, goats, and bison) and antlers of deer is that deer antlers are shed and regrown every year. Also, deer antlers are made of bony tissue, while the horns of bovidae are permanent, toughened bony structures. They grow only once. If broken, they do not grow back. Deer antlers become stronger and more branched with each year until they reach the full size of an adult. In old age, the antlers become weaker and somewhat smaller. This suggests that the growth of antlers is closely linked to the maturity and reproductive system of the male.

Red deer are social animals that tend to form two separate and different groups. One group is comprised of females and the young under the guidance of an adult female. The other group is formed by males that are at least three years of age. Like other species of social hoofed animals, the males live separate from the females. The groups of males are groups of individuals in which each member must fend for itself.

At the end of the summer and the beginning of fall during the mating period, the males with perfectly developed antlers enter the territory of the females. At this time, the males can no longer tolerate the presence of other males. Each male establishes a territory in which it tries to keep the largest possible number of females. The male declares its "territorial rights" with loud bellowing noises made at night. The female deer do not form any type of social bond with the male, though they do not resist the male's domination.

In this phase of mating, the males engage in frequent and violent battles to set up and defend their conquered territory. The antlers are not so much deadly "offensive weapons" as they are "tournament weapons." This is because the battles resemble ritual duels more than savage fights. Occasionally, during a battle, the antlers of two males become interlocked without seriously harming either animal. Sometimes it even happens that the males cannot separate their interlocked antlers. If this happens, they both may die.

The time the female will accept a male lasts no more than one month. During this time, no stag is able to keep a territory longer than one week. The continual fighting with rival males and the persistent state of excitation keep the male deer from eating. The male becomes so weak that he is physically not able to confront his rivals. Exhausted, he soon is forced to abandon his territory to a new male, retiring to quieter areas. He will remain here for a few days to restore his energy, eating large amounts of food. There he can build up enough energy to defeat a new rival and take possession of another territory.

The second of the original herbivores of the ancient deciduous forest is the roe deer. This hoofed animal is rather small, measuring about 27 inches (70 centimeters) in height at the shoulder, and weighing about 33 to 66 pounds (15 to 30 kg). It has a short tail, slender legs, long ears, arched back, and a coat of hair that is grayish in winter and reddish in summer.

This animal has adapted perfectly to an agricultural environment. Although its diet in the past was mainly leaves and plant stems, today it likes to feed on cultivated plants. Its daily activities are regulated to avoid human activities. The feeding trips into cultivated fields are made only at the earliest hours of the morning, the hours after sunset, and quick snacks at times when people are not near. The rest of the day and night, the roe deer remain hidden in the vegetation bordering the fields. The roe deer is the most common deer species in Europe.

The various populations of roe deer do not greatly

differ in their physical characteristics, shape and weight of the antlers, or behavior. They do differ in the color of their hair. Like all deer, roe deer lose and regrow their antlers each year. They are smaller and less branched than antlers of other deer but have the same functions. At three or four years of age, the male roe deer has completely developed antlers. The structure of the antlers can be modified by weather, wounds, or by hormones. The antlers may have outgrowths with rather interesting shapes.

The roe deer usually lives in small family groups that can combine in the winter into larger groups. However, this union of different family groups lasts only a short time. At the beginning of spring, the different families separate from each other to occupy a larger territory. This also is the time when the young males separate permanently from their mothers.

At the beginning of summer, all of the males begin to lead a solitary life. They carefully avoid other males and approach females that are not pregnant. As the female's estrus, or time of being "in heat," draws near (in July, August, or even late fall), the male roe deer cannot tolerate the presence of other males. The territory is marked by odors produced by glands in the front legs. Any other male that enters the territory is attacked with great fury. Sometimes this small deer, which normally is frightened and flees upon hearing the faintest unusual sound, will even challenge humans. It tolerates only the females.

In order to mate, the male must often follow the female for long distances across forests and cultivated fields. During this time, however, the female may suddenly flee. If mating occurs during the summer, there is a pregnancy of about nine and one-half months. During this time, the embryo remains dormant for about four and one-half months. If, instead, mating occurs during the fall, the pregnancy does not include a period of dormancy, and the fawn is born in about five months.

The third original hoofed animal of the forest is the wild boar. Its survival and widespread distribution is due mainly to its omnivorous diet. The wild boar eats both plants and animals. Its diet includes acorns, walnuts, mushrooms, beechnuts, broken ferns, small elderberry shrubs, roots, bulbs, and tubers. However, it also will eat worms, insect larvae, bird eggs, small rodents, rabbits, fish, snakes, and even dead animals. The wild boar can live anywhere, from North Africa to northern Scandinavia. Its northern

Below: A sow with several young wild boars (which still have striped coats of hair) wanders in a marshy area in northern Italy. Centuries ago the wild boar was extinct in many regions of central Europe. But in recent decades it has multiplied. It has even been reintroduced as a game animal for hunters in many localities that are similar to its original habitat. This hoofed animal is so adaptable that it has become a problem for farmers. It enters fields of corn and rice and knocks down large areas of plants just to eat a small amount of grain.

Opposite page: The large canine teeth of the wild boar are used as weapons in battles between males and as a defense against enemies. The male (lower drawing) has larger canine teeth and a bigger skull than the female (upper drawing).

limit of distribution seems to be determined only by the average depth of the snow.

Under severe winter conditions, the wild boar is forced to migrate over long distances, but in good weather, it remains within a definite territory. A territory has one or more small, marshy lakes. In the summer and in the mating period, besides drinking the water, the animals take mud baths. This practice is very useful in keeping the skin healthy.

The wild boar cannot see well, although it does have a very keen sense of smell, a good sense of hearing, and perhaps an ability to sense vibrations in the ground. In the males and to a smaller extent in the females, the lower canine teeth (the longest, sharp-pointed teeth) are peculiar. They stick out from the lips and are pointed upward. They

are slightly curved inward at the tip, forming a sort of tusk. The upper canine teeth are smaller. They are positioned in such a way that the smallest movement of the jaws causes a rubbing of the upper canine teeth against the lower ones. This results in the sharpening of the lower canine teeth.

The canine teeth of the wild boar are effective defensive and offensive weapons. They are used by the males especially during the mating season from November to January. In this period, the adult males, which normally lead a solitary life, seek out females in heat. The males engage in violent battles with rival males. These battles would be deadly if the shoulder region of the wild boar were not protected by greatly thickened skin that acts as a shield. This thick skin extends from the shoulders along the sides of the chest to the last rib.

The reproductive ability of the wild boar is linked to how much food there is in the habitat. In especially favorable years, half of the mature females will reproduce. In unfavorable years, however, it is possible that no females will reproduce.

The females normally live throughout the year in groups of one or more with their young. When they are pregnant, they leave the group sixteen to twenty weeks after mating and go to quiet areas that are rich in vegetation. Here they prepare the nest and give birth to six to eight young. During this time, the female becomes very aggressive against anyone or any animal that approaches the nest. Even male wild boars are not permitted near the nest.

Usually, the wild boar is not well liked by farmers because of the great damage it does to cultivated crops. Most of the damage is due to the animal's digging habits rather than the amount of plants eaten. In the woods, however, the wild boar is regarded as a useful animal. It destroys large amounts of insects that harm plants. Also, by their rooting about in the dirt, the soil becomes aerated or loosened. Seeds that have been buried too deep in the soil are brought nearer to the surface to sprout. In this way, the forest is renewed.

The damage to cultivated fields caused by wild boars could possibly be avoided without having to kill a lot of these animals. This might be done by taking advantage of the animal's keen sense of smell. For example, they cannot tolerate the odor of petroleum. In many cases, farmers could create an "odor barrier" around cultivated fields.

THE CARNIVORES OF THE FOREST

In the past, all of the species of herbivores described in the preceding pages were the favorite prey of the medium-sized and large carnivores, or meat-eaters. However, most of these predators have been hunted so much by humans that today they have totally disappeared from the forests of the central European plains. They have survived only in the mountainous areas. This has been true with brown bears, wolves, and lynx. Up to a little more than a century ago, these three large European carnivores dominated the forests of the European continent. They were considered to be dangerous wild animals.

The surviving carnivores of the forests of the European plains are small or medium-sized species. These include foxes, wildcats, and the weasel-like animals such as mink, martens, and badgers.

The Fox

Although the wolf has become rare today on the European continent, its close relative, the fox, has expanded into just about every type of habitat. These habitats include the agricultural areas where only a small amount of tree cover is available. Foxes have been found even in the urban area of London. Populations now live in the center of cities such as Oxford and Brighton, England.

An example of this animal's adaptive capacity is its flexible diet. Basically, the fox is an omnivore, feeding on fruit, insects, small mammals, bird eggs, and small domestic animals. For lack of anything better, the fox might fill its stomach with grasshoppers. However, when it can, it will kill a pheasant or even a small wild boar or a roe deer. It can go without food for quite a while. However, if food is abundant, it will kill many animals and bury them in holes dug in the ground for later feeding. The fox can easily find these hiding places even when snow covers the ground.

The size of a fox's territory varies greatly according to the amount of food. Those that live off garbage in suburban areas occupy territories of about 10 to 12 acres (4 to 5 ha). Those that live in the steppe need an area of 3,700 to 4,950 acres (1,500 to 2,000 ha) to survive. Foxes mark their territories with odors produced by the anal gland. It is believed that other glands located near the sole of the foot mark hunting routes.

The period of heat of the females is very short, not lasting more than thirty-six hours. Mating only lasts a few minutes, and it is similar to the mating of dogs and wolves.

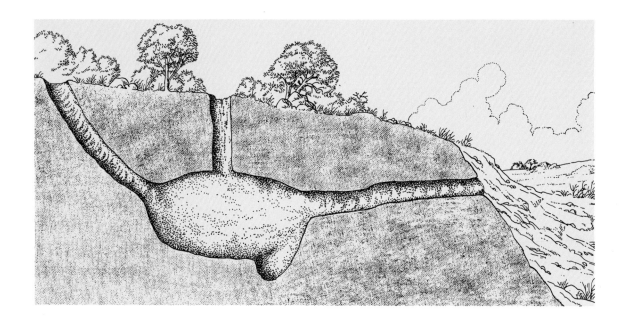

The male is polygamous (mating with more than one partner). Other males are absolutely not tolerated in the territory.

The dens are dug in sunny areas of the forest in soil that is dry, but not hard. Foxes often use the dens of other animals, especially those of badgers. The foxes and badgers seem to have a "truce" until the birth of the fox pups between March and April.

After a period of nursing and constant care of the pups, the mother pays less attention to them. Finally, at the end of August, the young have become independent. At this time, the adult males have begun to mark off their territories, forcing young males to leave the area of their birth. They usually must travel long distances to find unoccupied territories. Fortunately, the battles the young males have with other males are usually bloodless. They generally consist of vocal communication and aggressive postures.

The Wildcat

The European wildcat and lynx were both widespread in the ancient European forest. Today, the European wildcat inhabits the most remote and hard-to-reach areas of the Eurasian forests. There the wildcat is a skillful hunter of rodents, hares, rabbits, birds, and insects. It is active at night. During the day, it lies in the sun on tree branches and stumps.

The fox den is either dug by the fox or converted from the den of another mammal. The central chamber of the den is about 3 feet (1 m) in diameter, and it is located about 6 to 10 feet (2 to 3 m) below the ground surface. Several tunnels lead from this central chamber to various entrances.

This photograph of a wildcat was taken using a flash camera in a forest. There are few differences between the European wildcat and the North African wildcat. The domestic cat has characteristics that are intermediate between the two wildcats. Although this animal is rarely seen, it is fairly common in the three large southern European peninsulas and in the thickly forested areas of central Europe and Scotland.

The European wildcat is known to have a large body, a small tail and small ears. This form reduces heat loss in a cold climate. It is also covered by a thick coat of hair. It appears that the wildcat is strictly monogamous (mates with one partner). However, some individuals, perhaps males without a territory, lead a solitary life. The mating season begins in early March. At this time, the male starts to make loud, mewing sounds. Between April and May, the female gives birth to two to five young. Beyond this, the wildcat's habits and behavior are not well known. Its cautious nature makes it extremely difficult for scientists to approach.

The Weasel-like Animals

Other than the carnivores that have been described, the various members of the weasel family are the most characteristic of the European forests. Because of their different predatory adaptations, they occupy various environments.

With its 27-inch (70 cm) length and 22 to 44 pounds (10 to 20 kg) of weight, the badger is certainly the most unusual animal of its family (which includes mink, weasels, ferrets, and martens). Besides its stocky body, another feature of the badger is its way of walking like a bear. It has some social behavior, but each badger sharing a den lives in a manner that is independent of the others. It makes a variety of sounds such as puffing noises, moans, bellows, growls, and long yells, although they are rarely heard by people.

Although they are all carnivores, their diets include large amounts of insects and plants.

The badger, a stocky animal with a black-and-white snout, is primarily a vegetarian. However, it also eats bird eggs, young birds, small hares, and above all, rodents. It lives throughout Europe. The badger lives alone in dens at the edges of forests. The den is made in dry earth and has a main room, or chamber, that is generally 3 to 6 feet (1 to 2 m) deep. Many tunnels branch off from it, leading to entrances at the surface that are at least 33 feet (10 m) from each other.

The badger leaves its den only at night to search for food. In the winter, although it does not hibernate, the badger sleeps for long periods. It wakes up from time to time to leave the den to search for food. During the mating season, which occurs in summer, the male and female live together. After mating, the embryo does not begin to develop for four to five months. In February, the female gives birth to three to five young. It nurses and cares for them until the next autumn.

An interesting method of tracing the movements of badgers was recently used in a study made in Scotland.

The pine marten is easily distinguished from the stone marten by the yellowish patch under the throat (the stone marten has a white spot). The yellow is usually spotted with brown or is divided into two patches.

Food containing small, colored plastic balls was left in an area of the forest where a large number of badgers lived. These plastic balls, later found in the badgers' droppings, were used to map out the territory. Easy-walking badgers can cover considerable distances. They have been traced over four miles from the nearest feeding area.

The marten is very different from the badger. It is longer and more agile and slender. It is so skillful in moving among tree branches, that it is able to prey upon squirrels and birds. It also eats many insects, fruit, and berries. Watching a marten chase a squirrel is quite an amazing sight. The marten tries to block the escape of the squirrel by keeping it from climbing into the highest tree branches. The small branches are too thin to carry the weight of the marten. If the squirrel tries to escape by jumping to another tree, the marten will also jump. Its tail helps the marten keep its balance. After catching its prey, the marten bites through the vertebrae of the prey's neck to kill it.

The marten is highly territorial. Unlike the badger, this animal does not build a nest, but uses the nests of squirrels, crows, or ravens. Sometimes it even uses cracks in rocks or hollow tree trunks as a shelter.

SMALL MAMMALS OF THE FOREST

Despite the almost total disappearance of carnivores such as the wolf and lynx from the deciduous forest, there is still an animal world on a smaller scale. The world of the small mammals is characterized by complex relationships between prey and predators. An example of this has been described in the section on the marten. In this world, both prey and predators are fairly small, silent, and not often seen. Due to its liveliness, however, the squirrel is one of the few rodents that people enjoy.

The Squirrel

The long, soft S-shaped tail is the most interesting characteristic of this animal. It makes up almost half of the squirrel's length of approximately 18 inches (45 cm). The tail is used for balancing while the squirrel runs and climbs on tree branches. It even acts as a parachute when the animal jumps. At night, it is used as a blanket; during the day, it shields the animal from the sun. When eating, the squirrel rests on its hind legs and cracks open walnuts, seeds, and other foods, bringing them to its mouth with the front feet.

Squirrels mainly eat walnuts, hazelnuts, pine nuts, and acorns. They will also eat flowers, mushrooms, insects, bird eggs, and sometimes dead animals. They bury seeds and fruit near the trunks of trees, to be eaten later during winter. With their sense of smell, they are able to find this stored food even under a layer of snow. Still, some of the buried seeds are forgotten in the ground, so the squirrel helps plant trees and shrubs without knowing it.

Squirrels are very sensitive to the temperature of the environment. In the summer, they are not active at temperatures above 77° Fahrenheit (25° Celsius). In the winter, the squirrel does not go into a true hibernation. It takes shelter in its round nest, lined with moss, and rarely comes out in search of food.

The squirrel's coat is generally reddish except for the lower parts, which are white. In several regions where it is found, especially farther south, the squirrel can have a dark brown and sometimes black color. However, it always has white underparts. A dark red variety with an almost white tail is found in the British Isles. Tufts of hair at the tips of the ears grow in winter. In the summer, these tufts either disappear or are very small.

The mating season of the squirrel depends on how far north or south it lives. In the north, there is only one mating

Opposite page: A European squirrel shows typical reddish color. There are many species of squirrels throughout the world, but there are only three native European species. One of these lives in trees, and the other two are ground squirrels that are found in eastern Europe.

period, and it occurs in the spring. In the south, mating occurs twice yearly, once between January and April, and again between May and August. As soon as the young are born, the adult males are driven from the nest. The newborn young are blind and helpless. But after only six weeks, they are already able to make acrobatic trips outside of the nest. In addition to the common squirrel in the British Isles and in other European localities, there is another species of squirrel. This is the gray squirrel, which was imported to Europe from North America several decades ago.

This rodent is larger than the common European squirrel, although they are close relatives. The gray squirrel is less agile in the trees, but it is faster on the ground, where it spends a lot of time. It does not have the tufts of hair on the ears. Its gray coat of hair becomes grayish brown in the summer.

Usually, the gray squirrel is less timid than the common European squirrel. In North America, it is seen in many cities, both large and small. It is also found throughout the British Isles, where it has largely replaced the common European squirrel. The population of the common European squirrel was greatly reduced in this area due to an epidemic disease and because the European squirrel could not compete with the stronger and more adaptable American squirrel. Also, the gray squirrel does not become inactive in the winter, not even for a brief period. In the cities, this animal relies on its human neighbors for some of its food during the cold season.

The Dormouse

The dormouse is another agile and lively acrobat of the forest. It is as skillful a climber as the squirrel. It is able to make long leaps from one branch to another using its long tail for balance. It lives in forests, on the plains, and in the mountains. It prefers oak and beechwoods, and it is not found in conifer forests. The dormouse is a nocturnal animal, and like most nocturnal animals, it has very keen senses of hearing and smell. However, its sense of touch is the most developed of all. Besides having whiskers, it is equipped with sensory pads which are located in the skin of the face, on the jaw, and on the front legs. With these, it can tell where objects are in the dark.

During the day, the dormouse hides in a tree cavity or in a hole in the ground. Only at night does it come out in search of food. This animal has a large appetite. It eats

Opposite page: A young dormouse eats a cherry after recently waking from hibernation. By the time cold weather arrives in the fall, the dormouse will have stored a large amount of fat in its body to live on through the hibernation period. At that time, the dormouse has a round and stocky appearance, quite unlike the shape of the animal in this photograph.

Above: A dormouse rests in a tree cavity. Though it is almost invisible during the day, the dormouse can be found fairly easily in the forest at night. The best way to spot them is to point a flashlight toward areas where rustling sounds are made. Since dormice eat a lot of cultivated fruit, they have been widely killed in the past by farmers and hunters.

Below: The circular muscle, located just under the spines and the skin, allows the hedgehog to stick out its spines as it rolls into a ball. The spines are used mainly for defense.

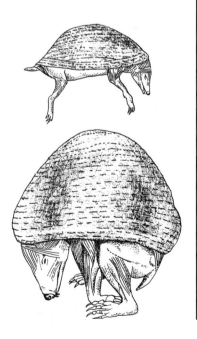

acorns, beechnuts, hazelnuts, chestnuts, fruit, and all the small birds that it is able to catch. In the fall, when the temperature is still far above 32° F (0° C), it goes into a den with one or a few other dormice and hibernates. The dormouse is probably the heaviest sleeper among the animals that hibernate. During the hibernation period it uses its stored fat for survival.

The main predators of this small rodent are martens, wildcats, skunks, and nocturnal birds of prey. In certain regions, people hunt the dormouse for its meat. This meat was considered a delicacy in ancient Rome, where dormice were raised and overfed for their food value.

Three other species of mice are found in the woods of central Europe. One is the garden dormouse, which has a small, black mask and a black-and-white, bushy tail. The tree dormouse has an appearance halfway between the dormouse and the garden dormouse. It has a black mask, short ears, and a bushy tail, but it is smaller than both and found only in eastern Europe. Finally, the hazel mouse is a tiny dormouse with a beautiful reddish golden color. The hazel dormouse constructs small round nests where several individuals spend the winter together.

The Hedgehog

Among the small mammals that live in the forests and countryside of Europe, the hedgehog deserves special attention. This animal belongs to the group of insectivores, or insect-eaters, which includes the most primitive placental mammals. Placental mammals nourish their embryos through the mother's uterus. They do not carry their young in a pouch. The hedgehog has a pointed snout that is similar to those of the moles and shrews, which also are insectivores. It also has small eyes and teeth, and it is best known for the quills that cover its back.

The quills are attached to the skin in such a way that they stick out when the skin is stretched. A large oval muscle under the skin contracts and allows the animal to change into a ball of quills. This adaptation is the only defense of the animal against any type of serious threat it may encounter. If the hedgehog is not greatly alarmed or threatened, it is able to raise only the quills in one or more areas of the back, leaving the others lowered.

This animal is not very sociable. It normally lives alone, using tree cavities and holes in walls as its shelter. It comes out in the open only at night to search for food. This is made

These two hedgehogs are slowly unrolling from the ball shape that they took after being frightened. These animals are rather slow when compared to most other small mammals. They prefer to roll into a ball rather than to flee. Because of this, hedgehogs are frequently run over by cars on roads in wooded areas. However, their numbers are not declining, since they are very adaptable and have many young. They are seen more and more frequently even within cities and smaller towns.

easier by its keen sense of smell. Its eyesight is not good. Even though the hedgehog is an insectivore, its diet also includes a wide variety of earthworms, snails, toads, lizards, small birds, mice (only small and diseased ones), shrews, fish, and poisonous animals such as wasps and vipers. The hedgehog has a remarkable resistance to poison. Scientists estimate it can stand seven thousand times more poison than humans.

Because of its excellent defense mechanism, the hedgehog is threatened by very few predators. They are attacked by birds of prey that have strong claws, foxes, dogs, and wild boars. However, its worst enemies are humans. The ancient

Romans used its quilled skin for combing wool. Up until only a few years ago in the Mediterranean regions, hedgehog meat was highly prized. People would cook this animal after having wrapped it in clay so that its quills would stick to the clay when it was thoroughly cooked.

Today, many hunters kill hedgehogs because of the animal's habit of eating the eggs of game birds that nest on the ground such as pheasants, grouse, and partridges.

The mating season of the hedgehog occurs in summer. During courtship, the male rapidly circles around the female and tries to calm and approach the female by spitting saliva. This saliva contains a pheromone, a chemical substance produced by an animal that influences the behavior of others of its species. Usually the female does not want to mate with the male and flees, forcing the male to repeatedly chase after her. This sometimes lasts for a good many hours, until they finally mate. This is the only type of social behavior for the hedgehog.

Shrews

Shrews are nocturnal insectivores with a widespread distribution. These animals do not hibernate in the winter but take shelter in houses, stables, barns, and silos. In the

A shrew cautiously comes out from its den among moss plants. Shrews are active both during the day and night, and they can be seen more often than other small mammals. They are quick and move excitedly. They stop suddenly and begin moving again immediately, vaguely similar to the movements of some reptiles.

summer, they prefer to live in the abandoned dens of martens, mice, and other animals.

Shrews are definitely not social, since they are very hostile toward others of the same species. Because of this aggressive behavior, mating is generally difficult. In order to mate, the shrews practice a long and complex courtship, stimulated by a strong odor produced by the glands. The young are born blind, hairless, and are totally dependent on the mother.

Strangely, these insectivores are preyed upon only by certain birds of prey, by storks, and by vipers. Wildcats kill them but do not eat them, and the weasel-like carnivores do not prey on them. A strong musk odor secreted by two glands located on the sides of the shrew's body discourages predators.

THE BIRDS OF THE FOREST

The relatively silent life of forest mammals is contrasted by the many sounds coming from the birds in the trees, shrubs, and undergrowth. The bird calls are used, above all, to signal the borders of their territories to other birds of the same species. This territorial defense is not just during the mating season. It is also necessary so that competition within the same species is kept to a minimum making sure that adequate food is available at all times. Some species, however, can have territories that partly or totally overlap with each other. They do not compete with each other because their diets are different. This is the idea behind the term "ecological niche."

Sometimes different species of birds are adapted to sharing the same habitat and the same food source. For example, soft invertebrates (animals without backbones), such as earthworms and insects, are the main food source of three different bird species. One is the thrush, which hunts in the upper layer of forest clearings. Another is the blackbird, which prefers the herbaceous undergrowth (non-woody plants) of the forest, but also hunts in the upper layer. The woodcock occupies an ecological niche similar to that of the blackbird. However, it searches for food just under the ground surface.

The Woodcock

The long beak of the woodcock is quite sensitive. Its many nerve endings help the bird find earthworms while searching through the decayed vegetation on the forest floor. It appears that the earthworms mistake the tapping of the woodcock's beak on the ground for the pitter-patter of raindrops. This sound stimulates them to move toward the surface, where they are promptly eaten by the woodcock.

The position of the woodcock's eyes is especially interesting. They are located toward the top and rear of the head. This allows the bird to see upward and backward while searching for food. Because of this feature, the woodcock does not have to interrupt its hunting to watch for enemies.

The woodcock spends most of its time on the ground, where it moves about quickly. Even the eggs are laid on the ground in a hole that is covered up with leaves.

The Pheasant and the Ringdove

The pheasant and ringdove are two other birds of the forest that feed entirely on the ground. Their diet consists mainly of seeds, especially cereal grains. The only thing

Opposite page: A well-camouflaged woodcock hides in the underbrush. This bird lives in open woods of broad-leaved and conifer trees with a dense, humid underbrush. The woodcock is related to shorebirds that inhabit shores and wetlands. It nests in hollows in the ground in forests of north-central Europe. It winters mainly in western and southwestern Europe and the Mediterranean area.

The pheasant is a beautiful fowl-like bird that originated in Asia. It was released as a game bird into Europe by the ancient Romans and Greeks. Unlike the partridge, the male pheasant mates with more than one female. The plumage (feathers) of the brilliantly colored male (shown in the photograph) differs from the speckled light brown camouflage-type plumage of the female. The showy plumage of the male attracts the attention of the female during courtship.

these two birds have in common is their diet. The ringdove is a tree-living bird which inhabits large forests of deciduous or conifer trees. The pheasant, instead, avoids forests of tall trees and prefers thickets of small trees and shrubs surrounded by fertile fields and grasslands.

The pheasant is a good runner but not a strong flyer. It roosts in trees only at a young age. Its nest consists of a hole dug in the ground and covered by twigs. This fowl-like bird originated in western Asia. Today, it is found in the wild in various areas throughout Europe. Its present widespread distribution is the result of its release by humans into many areas of central Europe. This releasing of exotic species is an old practice. It was done in ancient times by the Greeks and Romans, who highly valued its meat for food. Even today, the pheasant is considered an important game bird by many hunters.

Woodpeckers

In the forest, the songs of the birds are sometimes mixed with frequent drumming and tapping noises that might at first seem out of place. These are the sounds of a woodpecker at work on a tree trunk.

Woodpeckers feed on the many hidden insects that live in tree trunks, in cracks of the bark, and sometimes in tunnels dug in the wood. These birds have strong, sturdy beaks which are used to remove bark from parts of tree

Right: A female green woodpecker feeds facing its young in a nest hollowed out of a tree. This beautiful species inhabits forests of broad-leaved and conifer trees. It is easily recognized by the loud and shrill laughing sound that it makes.

Below: Like the feet of other climbing birds (parrots, for example), the characteristic feet of woodpeckers have two toes that point forward and two that point backward.

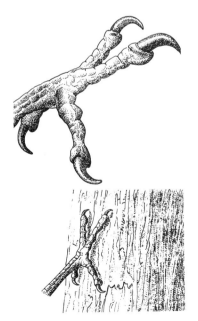

trunks, uncovering the entrance of insect tunnels. With its long, slender tongue, the woodpecker is able to catch and eat the insects that are hidden inside.

In addition to a well-adapted beak, woodpeckers also have several other characteristics. They can easily climb up tree trunks with the help of unusual claws that are curved like the steel spikes, called "crampons," used in mountain climbing. Two toes of each foot point forward, while the other two toes point backward. After each jump, the tips of the claws grip the wood or bark, while the bird's tail acts to balance and support much of the bird's weight.

The various species of woodpeckers drum and hammer according to their own distinct rhythms. The green woodpecker has an occasional, weak drumming. The black woodpecker drums constantly with a booming sound that can be heard over a half mile away. The greater spotted woodpecker taps less frequently with a rhythm of twelve to

sixteen pecks per second. In each case, the tapping functions as a territorial signal and as a call in the mating season.

Woodpeckers are normally solitary and aggressive. They make their homes in cavities of tree trunks, which are made into nests during the mating season. Modern-day forests are actually not ideal habitats for woodpeckers, since they are mainly made up of young trees. In the past, the older trees of the European forests provided more dead, wounded, diseased, or dried out trees in which nests could be made and food could be found. Also, conifer trees, which are now widely used for tree cultivation, are used only by the greater spotted woodpecker. The other woodpecker species are not able to tolerate the resin produced by these trees.

The European Nuthatch and the Short-toed Creeper

Besides the woodpeckers, the European nuthatch also is found on tree trunks. This perching bird is easily recognized because of its small size and great mobility. It runs sideways and up tree trunks. Unlike the woodpecker, it runs down tree trunks upside down. Its main prey are insects found on the surface of tree trunks. It also eats acorns and

seeds, especially those of beech trees, basswoods, and maples. To break open the shells of these seeds, the nuthatch inserts them into specially made holes in tree bark and repeatedly strikes them with its beak until they break open.

In building its nest, this bird uses clay or clayish soil that it wets and cements together with its sticky saliva. The mud is used to make a narrow opening to the nest to keep out intruders. The nuthatch is a social bird both in regard to its own species and to other species, especially the short-toed creeper and titmouse.

The short-toed creeper is another perching bird that feeds on the insects which live in tree trunks. It has a slender, curved beak which it uses like a pair of pincers for capturing insects among the mosses and lichen that grow in the cracks of tree bark. This bird is found in broad-leaved forests.

Titmice

Small birds called "titmice" are found in thick tree foliage, carefully searching their aerial territory for insects

Above: The flight of the short-toed creeper is wavy. The toes of this climber have slender, pointed claws. Like the woodpecker, it uses the rigid tail feathers as a support to easily climb tree trunks. It is also able to climb down trees upside down.

Right: A blue tit carries material to build its nest in a tree cavity. This small bird is one of the most common birds of the forests throughout all of Europe.

great tit

and larvae. The most common species in Europe is undoubtedly the great tit. In addition to forests, this bird also lives in gardens and city parks. Here it eagerly hunts insects and other small invertebrate animals including flies, millipedes, grasshoppers, bees, and wasps. It removes the stingers of bees and wasps before eating these insects.

The great tit is very curious, adaptable, and aggressive. A particularly intelligent titmouse in England learned to lift the tin foil cap off milk bottles left on the porches of houses in order to drink some of the milk. Soon this new habit became widespread among all the great tits of the same

population, spreading to nearby populations and passing to new generations. The birds apparently learned the trick by watching other titmice.

The blue tit, the coal tit, the marsh tit, and the crested tit also belong to the titmouse family and, like the great tit, they are found in forests throughout Europe.

The Jay

Many of the forest birds are specialized to take advantage of a rather small ecological niche. Others, instead, are very adaptable and get along well in almost any situation. The jay is certainly one of the most adaptable birds. It has light brown, black, white, and blue feathers. The jay eats acorns, hazelnuts, beechnuts, insects, lizards, and other small animals. However, it is especially fond of the eggs and newborn chicks of small birds. Even though it may kill some birds, the jay plays an important role in the growth of a forest. Most broadleaf trees owe their widespread distribution to the jay, which often "forgets" the seeds of trees which it buries. These buried seeds thus sprout much more easily than those that lie on the surface of the ground.

The call of the jay is one of the most characteristic and familiar sounds of the forest. Other than its harsh call of alarm, the jay also makes many other sounds including a variety of mewing sounds. The jay can even imitate the sounds of other birds. In captivity, it has been known to imitate human words with a pronunciation that is just as impressive as that of parrots.

Diurnal Birds of Prey

Only a small variety of diurnal birds of prey make their home in the deciduous forest. Diurnal birds of prey are those that are active during the day. There are actually only two common species, the goshawk and the sparrow hawk. These birds are perfectly adapted to the difficult conditions of hunting among the thick foliage of the forest trees. The sparrow hawk is rather small, while the goshawk is medium-sized. Their short, wide and rounded wings are designed to quickly reach a fast flying speed after leaving their roosts. They can easily maneuver in places where there are always many obstacles. This function is also helped by the long, wide, and very mobile tail. Their talons or claws are especially strong, which helps them to rapidly kill prey.

The sparrow hawk and goshawk are helped by the absence of other diurnal predators in the forest. They prey

From left to right: Shown are male and female hawks and male and female goshawks. These two species are closely related and are adapted to hunting prey in the forest. The males of both species are much smaller than the females. The male and female prey on different food resources, and they occupy different ecological niches (areas within a habitat).

on a very wide variety of birds and mammals. The males and the females of these species have different diets. This allows them to eat many different kinds of food available in the same ecological niche of the forest.

In both species, the male is much smaller than the female. The male sparrow hawk reaches a length of 10 inches (27 cm) and a weight of 3.5 to 7 ounces (100 to 200 grams) while the female reaches a length of 14 inches (37 cm) and 7 to 12 ounces (200 to 350 g). The male usually preys on small birds and mice while the female can prey upon birds the size of a thrush.

The male goshawk can measure up to 19 inches (48 cm) in length and weighs about 21 to 31 ounces (600 to 900 g). It can easily capture medium-sized birds such as jays or doves. The female goshawk has a length of 24 inches (60 cm) and a weight of 35 to 52 ounces (1,000 to 1,500 g). It can prey upon larger animals such as pheasants and hares with a good chance of success.

The honey buzzard is another bird of prey which nests in deciduous forests. It spends the winter in tropical Africa and migrates to the European forests in May. It reaches a length of up to 20 inches (50 cm) and a weight of 28 to 35 ounces (800 to 1,000 g). Despite its large size, this bird normally preys only on invertebrates and other small animals. Unlike other birds of prey, the honey buzzard

walks on the ground, where it often stays while digging for wasp nests. Its principal food consists of wasps and bees and their larvae, as well as honey. It also eats other insects, mice, lizards, and small birds.

A smaller species of falcon, the hobby, also makes its home in European deciduous forests. The hobby, however, is not easy to see. This bird of prey has reddish feathers on its legs and a striped belly. It mainly eats small birds. The male of this species is about the size of a female sparrow hawk, while the female is a little larger.

The Nocturnal Birds of Prey

At sunset, many animals seek shelters where they can spend the night. Meanwhile, other animals such as dormice, shrews, and small carnivores search for food. Even though the night seems still, many winged hunters lie in ambush of these creatures. The winged hunters belong to the owl family, and they are well adapted to life at night.

The plumage of these birds has a rather dull color, with patterns that perfectly camouflage them among leaves and bark during the day. Their heads are large and rounded. Several species have ear tufts. These tufts do not have a hearing function. They probably help the owl camouflage itself from its potential prey. The tufts interrupt the clearly curved outline of the head. This makes the head appear

Right: The long-eared owl is less common than the other owls. It lives in forests in both the mountains and plains. It becomes social during the winter.

Opposite page, from top to bottom: The drawings show the different appearances and body details of the long-eared owl. The ear tufts are fully erect while resting. The ear tufts are folded to the side when the owl is slightly alarmed. When it is fully alarmed, the ear tufts are folded against the head. The ear tufts of owls do not have anything to do with its sense of hearing. They function only as a camouflage feature. The wing feathers are frayed (fringed) on the outer edge, which allows air to pass by without producing any sound during flight. The sharp talons (claws) of the owl are long and very mobile. In the bottom drawing, the two feet are shown side by side as they are about to seize prey.

more irregular and helps the owl blend in with its environment. The eyes are very large and are located at the front of the head, giving them excellent vision. Owls are able to see the movement of a small animal on the ground even on nights without moonlight.

The precision with which these birds move from branch to branch is partly due to the sharpness of their vision and partly to their ability to memorize their territory. The memorization period is a long process which begins as soon as the young owl first leaves the nest. The adult owl is closely tied to its territory, since it is the only area that the bird has explored and memorized.

Even though owls may appear to remain motionless on a branch for long periods, they are always actively looking about for prey. An owl's head can rotate to 270 degrees or three-fourths of the way around on the neck. This adaptation makes up for the owl's inability to rotate the eyes. It also eliminates any noise that would be made if it were to move its body around on a tree branch.

Owls have very large ears covered by feathers which help them locate their prey with great precision. In some cases, the two ears are not the same size. This probably helps them hear more exactly where sounds originate in the environment. The fluffy feathers that cover the entire body of the owl (except for on the beak and the talons), reduce air friction. The wing feathers are fringed in such a way that the bird does not produce any sound while flying. This allows the owl to surprise its prey, without the least bit of warning of its arrival.

Once the prey is caught, the owl swallows it whole. The parts that are indigestible, such as bones, hair, and claws, are later regurgitated in small wads. Owls are able to do this by changing the direction of the contractions of their esophagus muscles. The esophagus is the muscular tube that moves food from the throat to the stomach. When zoologists study these wads, they can gather information about the areas of distribution of insects and rodents that are hard to trace by other means. They also can learn exactly what the owl eats.

The largest nocturnal bird of prey of European forests is the eagle owl. This bird reaches a length of almost 28 inches (70 cm). It can easily adapt to various climates and different environments. This feature allows the eagle owl to nest in forests, in steppes, and on rock ledges, from the Sahara Desert to the southern edges of the arctic zones. The mating season varies from the end of February to the end of April, depending on how far north or south the birds live. The female lays the eggs in large nests that have been abandoned by other birds of prey or else on the ground.

The long-eared owl is smaller, about 14 inches (35 cm) long. It is more slender than the eagle owl. It makes its home in the forest, but it also lives in areas with brush thickets between fields as well as in open areas with scattered trees. During the winter, it forms fairly large groups that inhabit undisturbed thickets on the plains, where it hunts rodents.

The tawny owl is about the same size as the long-eared

These two young "little" owls have recently left the nest. These adaptable birds live rather well even in the open countryside, nesting in old buildings and hunting insects and rodents. The little owl was introduced into England about a century ago, where it is now common.

owl

owl, but it does not have ear tufts. It is found in both dense and sparse forests. It has been seen in city parks and in attics of large buildings. It normally nests in hollow tree trunks. Since hollow tree trunks are not common in forests, the same tree may be used for many years.

The little owl is the smallest of the nocturnal birds of prey. The little owl and the tawny owl are the most common owls in Europe. The great adaptability which characterizes the little owl enables it to live in forests as well as in the open country, villages, and even some old houses in cities.

THE FORESTS BORDERING THE WATER

Bodies of fresh water such as rivers, marshes, and lakes create unusual areas of uniform environmental conditions called "biotopes." These areas have many kinds of animal and plant populations. A particular type of forest grows along riverbanks. This forest contains a variety of plant communities which differ especially in the species of trees that are present, such as oaks, elms, alders, and willows. A community is a group of species that live together in the same environment.

The presence of plants such as nettles, goutweed, and buttercups in the undergrowth indicates that the soil has a lot of nutrients and moisture. The soil is especially rich because of deposits of lime that accumulate during floods.

A Temperature-regulated Environment

In the past, large areas of forest grew along rivers and wetlands. Today, however, it is rare to find forests that have not been affected by humans. To take advantage of rich soils in river valleys, large areas of trees were cut down and replaced by rich, green pastures. Also, land reclamation projects which restored damaged land and the laws regulating the waterways added to the changing of these forests during the nineteenth century.

Even though the forests have changed, they are still the preferred habitats of many amphibians, reptiles, birds, and mammals. These include the animals that depend on water for their food and those that take shelter in warmer temperatures in the winter and cooler temperatures in the summer. In the environments along bodies of water, the air temperature does not vary so much from season to season. This is because the body of water has a temperature-regulating effect. Water gains and loses heat more slowly than air. Beavers, otters, and water voles are the most typical mammals of these environments.

The Beaver

The beaver is one of the largest species of rodent. It has evolved distinct adaptations to an aquatic life. The toes of the hind feet have large claws and are connected with skin. The second toe does not have this skin. Instead, it has a double claw which is used by the animal as a comb to clean its coat. The wide tail is flattened like a paddle, and it functions as a rudder during swimming. While underwater, the ears and the nostrils are closed by circular muscles called "sphincters." Even the mouth can be closed behind the

Opposite page: A beaver gnaws on a tree that soon will fall. The beaver has survived only in a few areas of Europe, including Scandinavia, Russia, along the Elbe River in Germany, along the Rhone River in France, and along the Versoix River in Switzerland. In many of these localities, the beaver has been released there to repopulate the area.

57

incisor teeth (the large front teeth) underwater, allowing the animal to gnaw or carry branches of trees. The beaver moves awkwardly on the ground, although it uses its front legs very well.

Beavers have an amazing ability when it comes to building. The most basic part of their complex constructions is the dam. Their dams create artificial lakes, where the water is kept at a constant level. The dams are built with tree trunks and branches, which may be taken to the water in special canals made by these animals.

The beaver builds a cone-shaped den in the small lake it creates, using branches and stones that are cemented together by mud. The outside of the den is reinforced by many branches, which make it look like a small island. The den has vertical tunnels with several entrances located below the surface of the water. Inside, the den is divided into several chambers or rooms. Some of them are used by the beaver as "waiting rooms" for their fur to dry, while others are used as "dining rooms." These chambers are connected to a main, or central, chamber of the den tunnels. The central chamber has a "chimney," a type of ventilation hole that allows air circulation. The floors of these little rooms are covered with wood chips.

The basic diet of the beaver consists of the bark of young twigs of trees such as willows, poplars, and others. In the summer, they also eat roots of water lilies, wood lilies, fruit, and herbaceous plants. These animals build underwater food storage areas which are used mainly to store food for the young during the winter. When cold weather sets in, the adult beavers eat very little and survive by using their stored body fat.

The reproductive period is from January to March. Courtship and mating take place in the water. From one to five clumsy young are born sometime between April and May. It is believed that the males are sometimes polygamous and that they establish stable relationships. Each beaver colony is composed of a mated pair and two generations of offspring. The number of animals living in a colony is rather constant, since young beavers are driven from the colony at two years of age. These young beavers, in turn, start their own colonies.

The work of beavers helps streams, especially in mountainous areas. The dams slow the rapidly flowing water, prevent the carrying away of sand and pebbles, and reduce floods. Other results of this damming activity are an

Opposite page: A colony of beavers works on a dam. The beaver is the largest rodent in Europe. An adult can reach a total length of 55 inches (140 cm) including a tail of 16 inches (40 cm). It can weigh as much as 44 pounds (20 kg). Several centuries ago the beaver was present in almost the whole continent of Europe. It lived in areas where rivers and lakes were surrounded by broad-leaved forests. The beaver was greatly hunted and trapped not only for its fur but also for an oily material called castor or musk, produced by special glands. The beaver uses the strong-smelling castor to mark its territory. Today the beaver is strictly protected by the laws of every European country.

Opposite page: A family of otters stands on the bank of a stream. These animals become wanderers except during the reproductive season. Otherwise they defend a vast territory that can include over 8 miles (14 km) of riverbank habitat. Groups of otters such as the one in the photograph are rarely seen now. Despite being adaptable and widespread, otter populations are quickly declining almost everywhere, due to trapping and water pollution.

Below: Several otters are busy with typical activities along the bank of a stream. At the left, an adult pushes a young otter into the water. Surprisingly enough, young otters are reluctant to jump into water for the first time, even though they will spend most of their lives in the water. In the center, another otter fishes under the water. Usually, otters catch fish that are not fast swimmers. To the right, there is a cutaway drawing of a den and its tunnels.

increase in the breeding area available for fish, the scattering of seeds of aquatic plants, the formation of wet meadows, and the growth of wetland forests.

The widespread hunting and trapping of beavers in the past has caused problems with the balance of nature and even economic losses to people. Eventually, these practices reached such a proportion that many governments decided to protect this species. Beavers were widely hunted for a number of reasons. In the Middle Ages, the official list of medicinal drugs included a remedy prepared with castor, a strong-smelling substance produced in the beaver's glands. The meat of the beaver also was valued. The tail, in particular, was considered a delicacy. However, the beaver was, and still is, most highly valued for its beautiful fur.

The Otter

This aquatic mammal has become quite rare in Europe. It lives in areas near fairly deep streams and lakes that have abundant vegetation. The otter has several mechanisms that enable it to live on both land and water. The eyes and nostrils are located toward the top of the head. The skull is flattened and the feet are webbed. When swimming, the legs are held against the body and the animal is propelled forward by a wavelike movement of the body. The

tail also helps this movement, and it also functions as a rudder.

When the otter is underwater, the nostrils and ears are closed and the muscles of the eyes adjust the eye lens so that the otter can see better. At night or in cloudy water, its vision is assisted by the sensitive whiskers of the snout. Its coat has long, thick fur that is waterproofed by oils produced by the skin. In the water, the fur flattens and offers little resistance. The fluffy hairs near the skin remain dry, and the air trapped by them acts as an insulating layer.

The otter feeds mostly on fish and sometimes on aquatic birds, water voles, and nutrias (aquatic rodents that resemble beavers). It is an expert hunter. It can swim faster than fish, so it can follow them for long distances. It may wait for them under a rock or surprise them with a lightning-fast dive. The otter may drive the fish into shallow water with movements of its tail. The fish are then easily caught. Sometimes this method is used by entire groups of otters.

The nutria has a length of up to slightly more than 3 feet (1 m) including a tail of 17 in (45 cm). It weighs 13 to 20 pounds (6 to 9 kg). It was imported in the past from South America, and it now is widespread in wetland areas of France, Italy, the Netherlands, Great Britain, Germany, and Scandinavia, as well as other countries. It is very graceful when swimming and diving. It digs very deep dens with an entrance that is partly under the water.

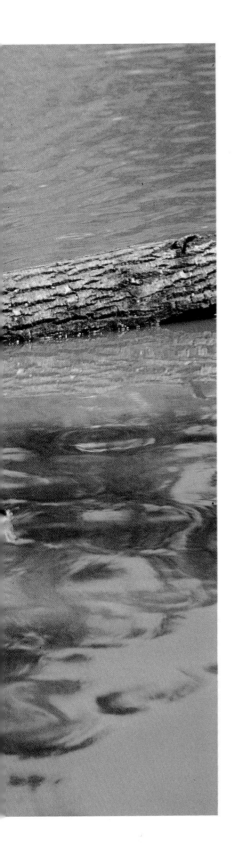

Generally, otters hunt against the water current and then let themselves drift back downstream. When hunting with the current, the otter covers most of the distance on land, zigzagging from one riverbank to the next.

The otter digs its den along riverbanks or lakeshores. The entrance is underwater, opening to a tunnel that leads to a large chamber lined with dried vegetation. This room has a small air tunnel to the outside. This animal is so well adapted to an aquatic life that it remains active even during the most severe winters. Then it makes holes in the ice and enters the water to hunt.

The reproductive period is from December to the beginning of March. During this time, the males search for the females by following trails of odors left by the females. The males call out to females with characteristic sounds and whistles. After mating, the male and female live together for a certain length of time. Pregnancy lasts about nine weeks, and the young remain with the mother about six to eight weeks. After weaning, the young start a training period. At the beginning, they are reluctant to jump into the water. Both the adults and the young spend a lot of time in games and playing. This is the main activity in which the otter displays its social behavior.

The Nutria and Water Voles

The original home of the nutria was Central and South America, where it inhabits riverbanks and lakeshores covered by aquatic plants. Because of its highly prized thick, soft fur, the nutria was widely hunted in the nineteenth century. Since the beginning of this century, the nutria has been successfully raised in captivity. Its present distribution in Europe is due to the escape of some nutrias from "ranches" where they were raised.

One of the characteristics of this aquatic animal is its webbed hind feet. The nutria feeds mainly on plants, although it also likes fish. Its diet is more similar to the diet of a rat than a beaver, which the nutria resembles.

Water voles are extremely aquatic. They prefer to live near streams, ponds, and cultivated fields with irrigation canals and ditches. Their diet consists mainly of plants. These animals cause large economic losses because of the amounts of roots and shoots of cultivated plants that they eat. Water voles are able to produce three or four litters of young per year. In favorable years, the population increases greatly.

FRESHWATER FISH

Besides hosting the various animal species which have already been described, freshwater bodies are also the undisputed reign of numerous populations of fish. The following fish are classified according to the physical and chemical conditions found along the rivers from their origin to the sea.

The Subdivision of the Streams

Necessary to the survival of plants and animals in the water is the presence of oxygen dissolved in the water. This gas comes either directly from the air or is produced by the leaves of submerged plants as a by-product of photosynthesis.

In the first section of a stream where the current is fairly rapid, the water surface in contact with the air is greater than the slower sections downstream. Thus, the water in the section of the stream near its origin has a very high amount of oxygen, which comes from the atmosphere. In other sections of the stream, most of the oxygen comes from aquatic plants. These plants do not provide as much oxygen as the air provides to rapidly flowing water. Since lower temperatures help dissolve oxygen in water, the waters flowing in cold environments are usually richer in oxygen.

The physical and geological conditions of an area affect the depth, temperature, and speed of stream water. So different sections of streams are inhabited by particular types of fish. In Europe, these stream sections are given names that correspond to the fish species that is typically found there. The borders of these sections are not exact and the same species can be found in the bordering waters of two different sections. The most accepted subdivision system names the first section of the stream, near the source, as the region of the trout. This is followed by the region of the grayling, the region of the barbel, the region of the bream, and finally, the region of the sturgeon.

The Trout Section

In the trout section of the river, the animals have adaptations to withstand the rapid water current and avoid being carried away and dashed against the rocks. Here, species of invertebrate animals cling to rocks, live in the slower water on the bottom, or are covered with natural or self-made armors to protect them from the impact of crashes against rocks.

The brown trout feeds almost totally on these inverte-

Opposite page: A salmon makes a spectacular leap as it swims up rapids. Some fish only live in a certain part of a river's length, but other species move from one type of environment to another. The salmon is an extreme example of this, taking a very long migration trip from the sea to the mountainous areas of a river.

65

A large male rainbow trout is seen in an aquarium, among vegetation that normally is not found in its environment. The specialists have found fifteen species and subspecies of European trout. The rainbow trout was introduced from North America in order to repopulate the streams.

brate animals. One of these, the river crayfish, is important because it causes the pink color of the brown trout's meat.

It is difficult to identify the brown trout species because it has many different forms and characteristics. This is from hybridization, or cross-breeding, and the actions of humans. It is almost impossible to decide exactly where subspecies, or varieties, live. The sea trout and the lake trout can be distinguished. Both of these subspecies migrate, one to the sea and the other to lakes. They remain in these areas for one or more years until it is time to reproduce. They then swim up rivers to deposit their eggs.

The river trout has a similar behavior, but, unlike its relatives, it always lives in rivers. The rainbow trout, which is from North America, is commonly found in European rivers. It can be easily identified by the pink stripe that runs along its sides. Europeans imported the rainbow trout because it can be easily raised. Large numbers of this fish

are released into streams for sport fishing. Other fish that inhabit the trout region include sculpins, minnows, and river lampreys.

The Grayling Section

The current is not as rapid in the grayling part of the river as in the trout section, although its waters are still cold, clear, and rich with oxygen. The most characteristic fish here, of course, is the grayling. The salmon, however, prefers this section during the reproduction period because it requires a higher amount of oxygen at that time.

The common Atlantic salmon, the only species of salmon present in European waters, remains in the rivers until two or three years after hatching, which occurs between April and May. After this two- or three-year period, in the month of April, the salmon join in large groups. Then they begin to swim down the rivers toward the sea. They stay around the mouth of the river for a long time. Here, they adapt themselves to the high degree of salinity (salt content) of the environment in which they will spend the future.

After a stay of two or three years in the sea, the salmon reach sexual maturity. They begin their migration to deposit the eggs in the river in which they were hatched. It appears that the salmon are able to recognize their native river through a highly developed sense of smell. This is believed to be true because salmon that have no sense of smell cannot find their way back to their native rivers.

The Barbel Section

The barbel section of the river has a deep and muddy bottom. Here, aquatic plants can grow well. Salmon cannot live in this section, but it is home for many types of minnows. The minnows are one of the largest groups of freshwater fish. There are over two thousand species. They have a toothless mouth, but they have bony formations in the throat that act to chew food. They are found from the barbel section to the sea.

Another inhabitant of this section is the pike, which is known as a fierce hunter. This fish helps keep the natural balance of the rivers in which it lives by eating other fish. This way, other species do not overpopulate the stream. However, it can become extremely damaging if it is released into waters in which it was previously absent. This is because the stream would already be in a balance without the pike.

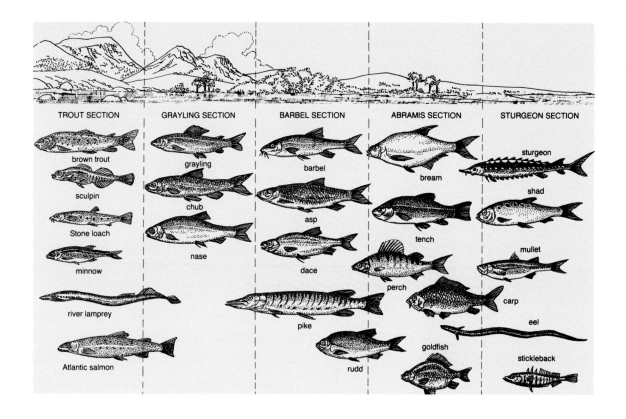

TROUT SECTION — brown trout, sculpin, Stone loach, minnow, river lamprey, Atlantic salmon

GRAYLING SECTION — grayling, chub, nase

BARBEL SECTION — barbel, asp, dace, pike, rudd

ABRAMIS SECTION — bream, tench, perch, goldfish

STURGEON SECTION — sturgeon, shad, mullet, carp, eel, stickleback

The Bream Section

In the bream, or Abramis, section of the river, the water is calm, warm, and often cloudy with abundant vegetation both on the riverbanks and on the bottom. In central Europe, the most characteristic fish of this zone is the bream, or *Abramis brama*, followed by the tench and the carp. The carp, originally from Asia, was released into Europe during the time of the Roman Empire.

The goldfish is another Asian fish which originated in Turkey and Mongolia. It was imported as an ornamental fish. Today, it is commonly found in many ponds, lakes, and in the lower parts of rivers. Its most unusual feature is the presence, in many European areas, of populations composed totally of females. These female goldfish are forced to mate with males of different species of carp. Goldfish are close relatives of carp. Although the sperm of the carp stimulates the fertilized egg to develop and grow, the genes of the males are not made part of the egg. For this reason, only female fish are hatched, and their genetic makeup is identical to that of the mother. This is called "gynogenesis." It is a particular type of parthenogenesis, which is the

A simplified diagram shows the distribution of several species of freshwater fish in the different sections of a river. In the trout section, where the water has the highest oxygen level, are trout, sculpins, salmon, and so on. In the grayling section are *Leuciscus cephalus*. In the next sections are fish species that do not require a large amount of oxygen. Near the mouth, the river becomes more complex, with more plant and animal life and different types of environments.

From top to bottom: During the mating season, the male stickleback builds a nest. He then attracts the female to lay eggs there with an elaborate and aggressive courtship dance. The male assists the female in laying the eggs by hitting her at the base of the tail with his snout. After depositing the eggs, the female leaves the nest from the side opposite where she entered.
Sometimes she is even driven away by the male. After this, the male takes care of the eggs. First he fertilizes them, then he creates a current to bring in oxygen by fanning his fins. This insures proper development of the offspring.

reproduction of organisms without the union of sperm and egg from a male and female.

The Sturgeon Section

At the mouths of rivers, tides cause the fresh water to mix with salty water. This zone is occupied by fish that migrate from rivers to the sea and from the sea to rivers. The migrating fish must spend a great deal of time adapting themselves to the different water conditions. Here, besides the salmon, are eels, the stickleback, and the sturgeon. The eels migrate from the rivers to reproduce far out at sea in the Atlantic Ocean. The young eels swim to the mouths of the European rivers by swimming upstream. They remain in the rivers until they reach sexual maturity. Then they migrate back to the sea.

The stickleback is about 3 inches (8 cm) long, and it has a very special social and reproductive behavior. During the winter, it lives in schools or groups in the sea and has a social type of hunting behavior. When one fish captures a prey, the others rush to take it away, tearing it to shreds in the process. These pieces of prey are shared by several fish. The fish that do not get any food react by hunting their own prey on the bottom.

The school separates in the spring, and the individual sticklebacks swim upstream in rivers. The male, which has bright colors, builds a nest. He cements together plant materials with a sticky substance secreted by the kidneys. Then he makes a tunnel through this nest with strong blows of the tail and fiercely defends his territory. In these territories, the males wait for the females, which swim around in groups, their bellies full of eggs.

The most spectacular fish of this section of the river are the sturgeons. After spending eleven to fifteen years in the sea, the sturgeons leave it to search for the river in which they were hatched, like the salmon. They spend about a month in areas with slightly salty waters. This change is necessary for the sturgeons since they must adapt to fresh water. Also, at this time, the fish develop their reproductive organs. The sturgeons then begin to swim upstream. When they reach waters with plenty of oxygen, each female lays about two million eggs. The eggs are then fertilized by the male. They remain attached to the rocks on the river bottom. People often collect sturgeon eggs, which are cleaned and salted and sold as caviar.

THE MARSHES

The marsh has always seemed like a dangerous and unknown environment for humans. The stagnant water, aquatic plants, diseases carried by swarms of biting insects, and the "poisonous air" people thought came from these places have helped to create a gloomy picture of the marsh for many centuries. For this reason, the government that promoted the reclaiming of agricultural land by filling in marshes tried to give the impression of fighting a major battle against the wildness of nature.

Now that these mistaken ideas have passed, the importance of learning more about the attributes of the surrounding environment has been discovered. This holds true even if the environment at first appears to be hostile to humans.

A Borderland Between Two Worlds

The marsh is a borderland between the terrestrial, or land world, and the aquatic world, a transition zone between two environments with very different characteristics. This makes it important in the study of ecology. The vegetation of a marsh produces an amazing amount of growth. As it was thousands of years ago, the marsh still is a safe refuge and a rich food source for hundreds of species of land and aquatic animals.

A careless observer would see the marsh as a disordered mass of more or less weedy plants located between the land and the water. Actually, the marsh is the result of a wondrous and difficult balance. The vegetation colonizes and fills in everything. The water, if its level rises, submerges all the plants and creates an open lake environment. Still, when untouched by humans, the marsh will evolve to the point of filling in completely, eventually changing into a forest. This process takes hundreds of years.

Beginning with the highest and driest areas and going at last to the submerged plants, a certain distribution of species can be observed. This distribution results from the adaptation of each species. In the areas where the ground is most solid, there are sedges, marsh marigolds, and horsetails. In the areas where water surrounds the plant roots, there are reeds and cattails. Water lilies float where the water is higher. Finally, there is the zone where the pondweeds grow at the surface of the water. Underneath, aquatic plants grow submerged. The microscopic green algae in the water harness the sun's energy and contribute to make the marsh one of the most fertile of ecosystems. This is shown by the number of fish inhabiting its waters.

Opposite page: A pair of snowy egrets flies from the water in a marsh environment. Herons, night herons, egrets, and bitterns are among the most typical and spectacular inhabitants of the wetlands, not only in Europe but all over the world. In Europe, the largest populations of these birds are found in the wetlands in central and southern Europe. In these areas, the rather high summer temperatures result in large numbers of small aquatic and land animals, which are the diet of these birds.

71

The courtship of the great crested grebe is very complicated and spectacular. In the "discovery" ceremony *(drawings 1, 2 and 3)*, one of the two partners swims under the water while the other bird positions itself to receive the swimming bird when it surfaces. In the "greeting" ceremony *(4, 5)*, the two partners first approach each other with beaks open and crests (feathers on the head) spread out. Then they raise their heads and turn their necks to touch their wing feathers. In the "plant" ceremony *(6, 7, and 8)*, the two birds swim under the water to gather aquatic plants, resurfacing with vegetation held in their beaks. They then swim toward one another with head low and neck outstretched. When they meet, the birds stand up like penguins, while hitting the water vigorously with their feet and moving their heads from left to right.

The marshy areas scattered along the edges of lakes, rivers, and coasts provide a habitat for grebes, herons, ducks, coots, geese, shorebirds, harriers (marsh hawks), ospreys, kites, reed warblers, great reed warblers, nightingales, and other songbirds. All of these birds find the proper environment in the marshes, where they build their nests and find their food.

Several delta marshes, which are marshes near the sea, are important stopover points for migrating birds. The destruction of a few coastal marshes of southern Europe would be enough to interfere with the lives of millions of birds. The balance that has been reached between the different parts of the marsh is quite delicate. This balance is easily upset by the pollution caused by humans and other outside forces. These environments thus require more care than other ecological systems.

French naturalist Jean Dorst stated, "The aquatic environments must, therefore, be protected as a whole from every type of abusive transformation. For centuries and centuries, humans have believed that it was best to dry them up, thus they destroyed entire biological communities. In

many cases, humans can usefully profit from marshy zones, conserving them as they are or rationally arranging them to increase the productivity of the habitat."

The Grebes

The grebes are among the bird species that are most typical of the aquatic environment. Their legs are short and located to the rear of the body. The toes have folds of skin called "lobes," that stick out while swimming. These help the grebe swim, but make walking on land difficult. The grebes are not good fliers. They cannot change direction very well, and taking off from the water is quite difficult for them. They drag themselves across the water for a certain distance, beating their wings before finally starting to fly. However, these birds are experts at swimming. They dive underwater with the greatest ease to capture small fish, tadpoles, clams, crayfish, and aquatic insects.

The largest grebe is the great crested grebe. It can be identified by its blackish ear tufts and dark chestnut feathers on the side of the head. Both the male and the female help in hatching the eggs and caring for the young. In the

The gray heron is the largest and one of the most widespread of the herons and egrets in Europe. Herons use different species of trees for nesting, as long as the trees are fairly tall and grow in undisturbed areas. In many areas with cultivated fields and nurseries, these birds cannot find the proper height of tree for nesting. In order to protect the herons, it is necessary to set up small nature reserves in which trees are not cut down.

first weeks after hatching, the parents carry the young on their backs. The young grebes remain there even when the adult dives underwater to search for food.

The European marshes are also inhabited by other species of grebes. The most common is the little grebe, which is small with a relatively short neck. It is a shy bird that prefers sheltered places. As soon as it comes out of a clump of reeds, it quickly dives underwater to escape being noticed.

Herons

Herons are wading birds that have long legs, long beaks, and long necks. Their diet consists mainly of fish, amphibians, crayfish, and clams. They hunt these animals in the shallow waters of canals, ponds, and rice fields. Here they can move easily because of their long legs. During their slow flight, the neck is bent in an S-shape.

Herons nest in colonies called "rookeries." These vary in size and can include up to one hundred pairs of birds. The nests are built in treetops in a disorganized fashion. Nests are of different sizes, and they are located close to each other. Several nests can be found in the same tree. The

An adult night heron rests in a marsh. It has the shortest neck of all the herons and egrets. The night heron migrates to tropical Africa during the winter. As soon as the young are on their own (July-August), they usually fly away from the nest in all directions, traveling distances of 500 miles (800 km) and sometimes even 745 miles (1,200 km). Besides living in the natural wetlands, all of the herons, egrets, and bitterns are able to find enough food even in rice fields. For this reason, they are commonly found in the Po River Valley, where there are many rice fields.

trees used for nests can be poplars, willows, alders, or even locust trees, as long as they are near water.

Nesting begins at the end of February. It continues throughout the spring as the herons gradually arrive from their wintering areas. A heron colony can be recognized by the continuous noise that these birds make, which can be heard up to a distance of several hundred yards. When the eggs begin to hatch, the activity in the colony becomes constant. The young are frequently fed. Their hunger is so great that the parents must make several trips each day from the nest to the fishing area.

One of the most widespread European herons is the gray heron. It is identified by its large size and gray color with black wing edges. This bird migrates from the northern Europe to the Mediterranean countries and Africa, where it spends part of the winter. During the winter, the gray heron is usually found in large groups in lagoons and marshes that are not too cold. The night heron and the snowy egret have similar habits. Many of them nest in the Po River valley of Italy.

However, not all the herons nest in colonies. The best

Right: The little bittern, with a length of 13 to 15 inches (33 to 38 cm), is the smallest of the European herons, egrets, and bitterns. In spring, the female (shown in the photograph) lays five or six white eggs in a nest well hidden among the reeds. Seven days after hatching, the young are already able to stand. At the age of twenty-five to thirty days, they leave the nest forever.

Opposite page, from top to bottom: A teal taking off from the water; a tufted duck taking off; a teal feeding; and a tufted duck feeding. The teal is a surface duck, flying directly into the air from its position on the water surface. When feeding, the surface ducks always remain at the water surface, with the tail pointing upward out of the water. The tufted duck is a diving duck. Before rising off the water in flight, it must first skim across the water for a certain distance. Diving ducks dive totally under the water while feeding.

known of the non-colonial herons is definitely the European bittern. This large, solitary bird builds its nest in sheltered areas among clumps of reeds in the midst of thick vegetation.

Ducks, Geese, and Swans

The best-known birds of marsh environments are not grebes, herons, or bitterns, but rather ducks, the webbed-foot aquatic birds. Ducks can be divided into surface species and diving species. The surface ducks live mainly in slow-flowing waters, ponds, and shallow marshes. Here they feed by dipping the top half of their bodies underwater. The diving ducks, instead, search for food by completely diving underwater, often going very deep.

The most common and widespread surface duck is the mallard. Its beak is long with a flattened tip. The edges of its beak have a row of bumps similar to teeth. With this beak, the mallard sifts and filters the muddy bottom, feeding on plants, shoots, and algae, as well as clams, insects, and insect larvae.

The northern ducks migrate south for the winter. Some of the central European ducks remain in the same area, and others migrate. The mallard builds its nest almost anywhere, hidden among the vegetation, usually near water. In the north-central countries, mallards even build nests in the trees of city parks. The female lays eight to twelve eggs. When the ducklings hatch, they are already able to walk behind the mother.

One of the most common diving ducks is the tufted duck. It is easily identified by the plumage on its back (black in the male, dark brown in the female, while the sides are light colored), a rather stocky body, and a small tuft of feathers on it head. This duck lives in large groups, often in the company of other species of ducks, in rather deep lakes and marshes. Occasionally, it can be found in rivers or estuaries where the rivers meet the sea.

The European pochard duck is often found with the tufted ducks. The males have light gray bodies, while the females are grayish brown. This diving duck prefers fresh-water environments. It nests in the reeds at the edge of calm water that is not too deep. This pochard duck is omnivorous, although it prefers to feed on plants. It is found in large flocks that sometimes include other species of ducks when it migrates and molts its feathers.

Geese are found in open fields and marsh environ-

A male and two female mallards float on a pond covered with aquatic plants. The mallard is a very common duck that not only is found in lakes, ponds, and marshes, but also in small bodies of water, even in city parks. This species is also commonly raised as a domestic animal. Sometimes wild mallards mix with domestic mallards.

greylag goose

white-fronted goose

Anser arvensis

lapwing

ments, where they feed in large flocks. The several species that are found in Europe generally resemble each other. These include the greylag goose, the white-fronted goose, and others.

The swans are found farther north than the geese with the exception of the mute swan, which also is the best-known species. Its distribution is centered around central Europe from northern Italy to the British Islands and from southern Sweden across Switzerland, Austria, Germany, Poland, and the Netherlands.

Rails, Gallinules, and Coots

This is another group of birds that is typical of aquatic environments. They generally have long legs and toes which help them walk with ease over floating aquatic vegetation. Their bodies are narrow, allowing them to easily move between the reeds. Their thick plumage protects them from the water and from cold temperatures. They are not good fliers, even though they can fly long distances. Normally, they fly only when they are surprised, escaping to the nearest safe area.

The European coot is the most common of these birds. It is easily identified by its grayish black plumage, which contrasts with the white beak and a hard plate about the beak called a "forehead shield." It has rounded feet like the grebes, which help make it an excellent swimmer. The coot does not hesitate to dive deeply in search of food. Its diet consists of aquatic vegetation, clams, insect larvae, small fish, and other kinds of small animals. This bird can be considered a true opportunist, since it is always ready to take advantage of the most common food. During the spring and summer, when it nests, it lives in small family groups. In the fall and winter, it unites in flocks of hundreds and even thousands of coots in areas of open water.

The Florida gallinule is smaller than the European coot. It has brownish olive plumage on the back, and a dark gray belly and sides. The forehead shield is reddish, and the beak is pure red with a yellow tip. Although the gallinule is a good swimmer, it does not have rounded toes so it rarely dives. Usually, it walks over the floating aquatic vegetation. Besides ponds and marshes, it is also found in stream areas where there is only a small amount of water. It has been known to colonize in cultivated fields, where it finds abundant food. In several countries, the gallinule is even found in city parks, where, like the sparrows and pigeons, it

A mute swan flies over a lake. These spectacular birds easily reach a weight of 22 to 24 pounds (10 to 11 kg). Because of this weight, they are able to take off only after flying just above the water surface for quite a distance. Once they have risen into the air, they become just as graceful as they were when swimming on the water surface.

sits on park benches, seeking handouts from people. In the winter, it often forms large flocks that can cause a lot of damage to fields.

Shorebirds

The term *shorebirds* is used for birds that have features that adapt them to environments of riverbanks, lakeshores, and even ocean shores. Besides these environments, shorebirds also can be seen in partially flooded fields, rice fields, and wherever there are open areas with muddy soil.

Shorebirds have legs that are long in comparison with the body. This allows them to easily move over land that is covered with water. When they search for food, the beak, which can be quite long, is placed completely under the water or mud. The structure of the beak determines the ecological niche of the various species. Several, like the curlew, with its long, curved beak, are adapted to hunting for crayfish and worms in the deep mud. Others, like black-tailed godwits, avocets, and pied stilts, have rather long necks and beaks. They search for food in areas where the

The great reed warbler signals its territory within the marsh with a loud, rhythmic call that sounds more like an amphibian than a bird. Like many other songbirds, it is more easily heard than seen.

European coot

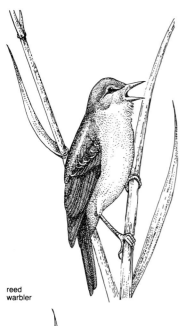
reed
warbler

marsh warbler

water is only a few inches deep. The greenshank is typically found on limestone banks and reefs that are covered by shallow water. It hunts amphibians, crustaceans, clams, and small fish by sticking its beak here and there in the water. Other shorebirds include lapwings, golden plovers, and other plovers.

Small Perching Birds

The wetlands offer a variety of environments that are suitable for the nesting and feeding of small perching birds. The nests of several small warblers can be found in the reeds at the edges of lakes and ponds, where the vegetation is the thickest. One of these birds, the reed warbler, is especially found in reed-grass vegetation. It builds a nest by weaving the plant's leaves and stems around the bottom of the stalks, which support the weight of the nest.

The greater reed warbler is also found in this area. This bird is similar to the reed warbler but is larger. It can nest in a greater variety of reed plants. It searches for food in other areas, such as drier brush areas. Also, its diet is more varied, including large beetles and large dragonflies, as well as smaller insects.

Other small warblers that are well hidden among the vegetation include the marsh warbler and the grasshopper warbler, which make sounds similar to the chirping of an insect. Also found in this area is a species of marsh bunting that builds its nest either on the ground or among the sedges and reeds, but sheltered from the water. This bunting prefers to feed on seeds of marsh plants. However, during the reproductive season it also eats insects.

The penduline tit and the bearded tit are beautiful perching birds that live in reeds. Their area of distribution is primarily in southern and eastern Europe, and only a few are found in central Europe. The white wagtail is found in marshy areas, and it also adapts to field and city environments. However, it is most commonly found along riverbanks. The gray wagtail is found in fewer types of environments. It is more associated with rivers and white-water streams containing an abundance of vegetation.

Birds of Prey

The abundance of prey in the wetlands solves the food problem for several daytime birds of prey. This abundance of food is especially important during the raising of the young which need a lot of food.

black kite

marsh hawk

short-eared owl

The black kite is the most adaptable, common, and widespread of the diurnal birds of prey that are found in aquatic environments. It is identified by its slightly forked tail. It lives near wooded areas and builds its nest close to lakes, rivers, and marshes. It beats its wings slowly while flying, taking long glides. It generally soars at high altitudes, flying in large circles.

The black kite feeds mainly on small and medium-sized prey. It also acts as a scavenger, eating anything it finds, including garbage. It picks up dead or dying fish from the surface of the water or from lakeshores. Because it will eat almost anything, the black kite has survived changes in its environment. It is now one of the most common species of its group.

Unlike black kites, male and female marsh hawks (harriers) do not have similar colors. The male marsh hawk has a fairly uniform gray color, while the females are mostly brown with dark stripes. Marsh hawks can be found near lakes and marshes, as well as in open moors and cultivated fields. The female lays three to six eggs in a nest hidden among reeds, and can raise many young. During the mating season, the male and female marsh hawks fly upward to great heights, making swaying movements while coming down, and then repeat the pattern.

The short-eared owl is another inhabitant of marshy areas, where it nests among the reeds. Although it is primarily a nocturnal bird of prey, this species also hunts during the day. Since the short-eared owl does not move about much at night, it is not necessary for this bird to memorize its territory, as is necessary for the long-eared owl and the tawny owl. Because of this, the short-eared owl lives in more open areas. Its hunting success depends on the abundance of prey. Its call is so unusual that it confuses people that hear it for the first time. It sounds like a sneezy bark.

Amphibians and Reptiles

The marshes, ponds, and oxbow areas (old river bends, now closed) are ideal environments for many small animals. These include amphibians and certain reptiles, as well as many invertebrate animals. Amphibians must deposit their eggs in water, where their tadpoles (larvae) live after hatching. The eggs and tadpoles are sensitive to water pollution. The survival of amphibians depends on the availability of clean, non-polluted water.

The European amphibians can be divided into two

warty newt

smooth newt

Lessona frog

green toad

common
tree frog

groups. The first group includes frogs, toads, and tree frogs, whose adults have no tails. The second includes tailed amphibians such as newts, salamanders, and olms, which are cave-dwelling salamanders. The two groups have other differences besides the presence or absence of tails. These include the size of their hind legs, the diet of the larvae, and differences in growth and development.

All of these amphibians deposit their eggs in the water. After hatching, the young, which have gills for breathing, spend the first part of their lives in the water. After metamorphosis (the change from tadpole to adult), only the typical frogs remain in the water to live a truly amphibian life. Tree frogs, toads, and salamanders leave the water forever. The tree frogs go to live on the branches of shrubs and trees, while the toads and salamanders live in shaded areas with many hiding places. The newts spend their adult stage divided between the water and land. The adults spend the winter buried in mud or moist soil. In the spring, all of the amphibians return to the water to deposit and fertilize their eggs.

The most common newts are the warty newt, the smooth newt, and the marbled newt. The most common frogs are the Lessona frog, 1 to 3 inches (4 to 7 cm) long with white vocal sacs, the laughing frog, 3 to 6 inches (8 to 15 cm) long with dark gray vocal sacs, and the aquatic or European edible frog, a hybrid, or cross, of the previous two frogs that has characteristics from both.

Various species of toads are found throughout Europe, including the common European toad, the natterjack toad, and the green toad. There are only two species of tree frogs —the central European tree frog and the Mediterranean tree frog. These two bright green frogs look very similar.

Because they reproduce in water, all of the amphibians have been affected by water pollution. In several cases, they have suffered large declines in numbers. The amphibians most affected are those that live in the plains, such as the newts and the European spadefoot toad, which is seriously threatened with extinction.

Environments that are close to streams and marshes also are preferred habitats of another group of small animals. These are the reptiles, which do not need to reproduce in water. Reptiles are not as common in central Europe as they are in the Mediterranean Sea. There is not a wide variety of species.

Very typical and widespread is the green lizard. This

European green frogs, unlike red frogs, do not have any trace of a "mask" around the eyes and have vocal sacs that puff out at the sides of the mouth in the males. There are three species of green frogs—the laughing frog, the Lessona frog, and the European edible frog. These last two frogs have the same distribution and are found in the same ponds. Recent studies show that the European edible frog (pictured here) is actually a hybrid cross between the laughing frog and the Lessona frog.

animal has a green body and blue throat. Its average length is about 5 inches (13 cm), but it sometimes reaches a length of over 15 inches (40 cm). It frequently digs long dens in riverbanks, never going more than about 10 feet (3 m) from the entrance to hunt for insects. The European fence lizard is similar to the green lizard, though it is smaller at about 3.5 inches (9 cm) and browner. In the cooler environments of Austria, Germany, and other central European countries, it takes the place of the green lizard.

The slowworm is a very strange lizard, since it has no

legs. This reptile has a long, thin tail and a small head. Its small eyes have movable eyelids, like most lizards. The slowworm grows to about 12 to 16 inches (30 to 40 cm). It lives hidden in wet fields and under rocks. It mainly eats snails. It gives birth to its young rather than laying eggs.

The most common central European snakes are the water snakes, which reach an average length of 40 to 60 inches (100 to 150 cm) and are excellent swimmers. Unlike lizards, snakes do not have eyelids, but a clear scale protects the eye like a swim mask. One species of water snake hunts mostly amphibians. Another species likes small fish, so it lives near larger bodies of water. In spring, these snakes mate in large, complicated tangles. They rarely bite even when teased, and the bite is harmless. To defend themselves, they release an unpleasant odor from their bodies.

The Aesculpian snake is also found in moist forests of central Europe. It reaches a length of 60 to 80 inches (150 to 200 cm). It easily climbs trees, where it preys on small birds and eggs. It also enters dens of small mammals to capture both young and adults. It kills its larger prey by constriction (squeezing). The prey is swallowed whole, which is a common practice with all snakes. Its back has a beautiful greenish and yellowish brown color with small light spots, while the underside is almost totally yellow.

One of the smallest snakes in Europe is the smooth snake, which sometimes resembles a small viper. Actually, the non-poisonous snakes, such as the smooth snake, are easily distinguished from the poisonous vipers by several features. For example, the head of the non-poisonous snake is covered by large, even scales, its eyes have round pupils, and the nose has a rounded shape. Finally, the non-poisonous snake's body is slender with a rather long tail.

The smooth snake is brown. On the average, it is 20 to 24 inches (50 to 60 cm) long, but it sometimes grows up to 31 inches (80 cm). This snake only hunts lizards.

The European viper is the most common viper in central Europe. It lives in drier moors as well as marshes. It hunts at night, using its poison fangs to kill rodents, birds, lizards, amphibians, earthworms, and slugs. Its bite is dangerous to people and requires quick medical attention.

THE COUNTRY AND THE CITY

The environments in Europe from the Neolithic period (about ten thousand years ago) to the present have had a constant decline in their forests and marshes, and a gradual increase of the cultivated steppe produced by humans. This environment is characterized by areas that are completely open and treeless, and other areas where trees are grown in rows that are spaced from each other.

Besides these landscapes, which are usually referred to as the "country," there also are city landscapes where the changing of the environment has been very great. In cities, the land is completely covered by buildings, roads, factories, and electrical wires. It is densely populated. However, even here one can find a number of animal species.

Birds of the Cultivated Steppe

The larks are a group of basically terrestrial birds that have gone along with the growth of the cultivated steppe. They are noted for their loud and melodious singing. They sometimes fly so high that people can hear their singing without seeing the birds.

The larks live in open areas and nest on the ground in fields of grain or in uncultivated fields. They migrate southward in the fall, wintering in large fields that are either plowed or left with the stubble of plant stalks. They winter from Scotland to Spain and Greece. These birds avoid the regions having a harsh climate, where the cold weather would make it difficult to gather enough food for survival.

There are many species of birds that live in cultivated areas, but not all of them are as closely connected with the open spaces of grain cultivation as the larks. Most birds of the crow family prefer environments consisting of large cultivated areas, which also have rows of trees and a few small wooded areas.

The crows are medium- or large-sized birds with an omnivorous diet. They are able to eat almost any kind of food, from live animals to eggs that are stolen from nests. Crows eat the flesh of animal carcasses, seeds, grains, sprouts of grains, roots, and whatever other type of food may be abundant. The presence of garbage on the edges of cities attracts large groups of crows. Here they hunt mice or search for food scraps. Their nest consists of a platform made of woven twigs and branches. These nests are built high into trees. Common crows show a social type of behavior when they build their nests in colonies. Depending upon the number of pairs in the colony, one or more trees may be occupied.

Opposite page: Stork nests are seen on tops of houses in Kupinovo, Yugoslavia. Generally, animals and humans live together peacefully in many cities, where people soon learn to respect the wild animals. Sometimes people help the animals in the different phases of their activities, such as building platforms for storks to nest on.

A flock of starlings darkens the sky during a winter sunset. On winter evenings, several European cities are invaded by tens or hundreds of thousands of these birds. At night, they need to take shelter from predators. At dawn, they flock back to the countryside in search of food. When the sun goes down, they return to the cities. The continuous chirping of these birds at night in the city and the large amount of bird droppings that accumulate cause a large problem for people.

Two types of carrion crows can be found in Europe, and they are distinguished by the colors of their plumage. The black carrion crow is completely black, and it is found in the western European countries of Spain, France, Portugal, and part of Germany. It is similar to the common crow except for the base of the beak, which is dark instead of gray. The gray carrion crow is easily recognized by the gray color of its back and lower parts, which contrasts with the black tail and wings. It lives in areas of central and eastern Europe.

The social behavior of the carrion crows is not as

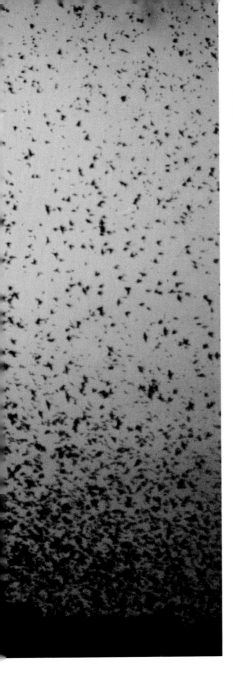

specialized as that of other crows. The mated pairs remain together for life, building the nest together, and joining large groups only after the reproductive season. When they migrate in the fall, they form large flocks with common crows. Sometimes several hundred crows can be counted in just one group. When one of these flocks stays in a cultivated field, a lot of damage results, especially to seeds that are germinating (sprouting).

The black-billed magpie is closely related to the crows and the carrion crows. It has bluish black plumage, a black tail and wings with bluish reflections, a white belly, and a long, tapered tail with green reflections. Magpies are found in open environments, whether cultivated or not. The magpie builds its nest in single trees, covering the nest with a roof of small twigs. In many European countries, this bird can be found in residential neighborhoods throughout the city. It moves on the ground with the same quickness as the carrion crows, walking and hopping like the jay.

It is necessary to mention the common starling when speaking about the birds that have successfully adapted to open environments. This is a plump bird with dark, speckled plumage and shiny blue-green reflections. It is easily recognized while flying because of its short tail and pointed wings. It alternates rapid wing beats with long glides, moving quickly through the air in a straight flight pattern.

The starling is a noisy bird which makes a harsh call, especially in the spring. This bird, which is commonly seen on roofs while calling loudly and flapping its wings, is found almost everywhere. It builds its nest in any cavity or enclosure with a wide enough entrance hole. It does not hesitate to invade the territory of other birds, driving away those with which it competes for nesting sites.

The starling was originally a bird of the steppe. It feeds on plants including berries, seeds, fruit, and sprouts, as well as on small animals such as insect larvae, snails, and clams. In the spring, the young are also fed with these small animals. The starling can use its strong beak as a pick to move dirt while searching for food.

Another reason for the success of this species is its social behavior. It has a strong group instinct, and when autumn approaches it unites in large flocks that contain up to several thousand birds. It migrates over rather short distances. Starlings living in northern territories migrate southward, while the southern populations migrate briefly in

A male gray partridge stands alert in a typical open environment. In the areas where this species has adapted to changed environments and to hunters, the males pair up with the females from February to May. After hatching the young, they remain in a family group for the rest of the year. They typically live on the ground and are well camouflaged among thick vegetation.

search of areas that have abundant food.

At dusk, the flocks gather in areas to rest for the night. In the morning, they can easily be seen flying from the countryside back to the city. Gathering into flocks helps them adapt, especially in searching for food. In winter, food can be abundant, but it is only found in certain areas. The fortunate starlings that have eaten an abundant amount of food during the preceding day act as guides for the other starlings by leading them to the newly discovered food source.

Starlings can cause serious damage to crops. Farmers use different methods to guard against invasion of these birds. These include scarecrows, nets, traps, alarm devices, guns, explosive charges, poisons, and even sounds amplified through loudspeakers. However, methods that come from scientific studies of the starlings' behavior get the best results. These methods use realistic models of starlings along with recordings of the starling's cries of alarm and fear. Still, the starling population is expanding.

Not all bird species have been able to adapt as well as the starlings and carrion crows to the environmental changes.

The gray partridge is an example of a completely different situation. This beautiful bird originally lived in the steppe. Today, however, it lives and nests in cultivated areas that are separated by rows of thick hedges and bushes. The gray partridge is monogamous and stays in its chosen territory from the moment it mates. It does not venture far from its territory, not even during the fall and winter. It lives in groups until February or March, when each mated pair separates from the group to hatch and raise the young.

The gray partridge has become an endangered species because there are no longer enough insects in its habitat. The chicks of the gray partridge must be fed with insects for about two to three weeks after hatching. Due to the widespread use of insecticides by humans, insect food has become scarce. Also, modern methods of farming have destroyed a large part of the hedges and bushes in which gray partridges nest. The result has been a steady decline in the population of this species. Since this bird is highly valued as a game bird for sport hunters, there is presently an attempt to use farming methods that do not harm this beautiful species.

However, no one has spent much time studying the decline of another fowl-like bird, the quail. This bird is much smaller than the gray partridge. Unlike the gray partridge, the quail migrates. This attractive bird has become quite rare today among the fields of grains that used to be its preferred environment. Even the decline in the population of this species is probably caused by the widespread use of insecticides.

Birds of the Wooded Countryside and Gardens

The hedges, thickets, and small uncultivated patches that separate the various agricultural fields are the ideal habitat for quite a number of species of small birds. These birds are very adaptable and can also easily live in city parks and gardens. Some of the best-known birds of this group are blackbirds, robins, nightingales, wrens, tits, shrikes, golden orioles, chaffinches, greenfinches, goldfinches, and cuckoos.

The blackbird and robin are found in nearly all the parks and gardens of Europe throughout the year. It is impossible not to notice them. The blackbird is dark and plump, while the robin is smaller and has an orange breast. They both have pleasing calls, which are heard in spring and winter. Another melodious songbird is the bucket

thrush, which nests in the parks and gardens of all the large central European cities.

The chaffinch is a small bird that is present throughout the year in various environments of the entire continent of Europe. Other members of the grain-eating finch family include the well-known and beautiful goldfinch and greenfinch.

Some of the "summer visitors" are the timid nightingale, the golden oriole, and the noisy red-backed shrike. All of these birds, which are quite different from each other, reach Europe in April or May, migrating from Africa. They reproduce in Europe and leave for Africa again in August or September. Nightingales are small birds with a dull brownish color. But their song stands out as the prettiest of all the birds.

Golden orioles are about as large as blackbirds, with showy black-and-red colors in the male, and greenish yellow and brown colors in the female. Like nightingales, golden orioles are not easily seen. They can be detected by the song of the male, which is a characteristic two-toned whistle that resembles sounds heard in a tropical jungle.

Nightingales and golden orioles prefer the moist plains, where they inhabit every thicket that offers enough shelter. The shrikes are found in the hills and are usually seen out in the open. Nightingales mainly eat insects, while the golden orioles also eat fruit. Shrikes even hunt small vertebrate animals.

Other summer visitors are the well-known cuckoos and hoopoes. The hoopoes are easily identified by the crests of feathers on the tops of their heads, brownish pink body colors, and white-and-black bands on the wings and tail. The beak is long and curved downward. Hoopoes stick their beaks into the soil to capture mole crickets, beetles, and insect larvae.

The cuckoo is a timid bird that is rather hard to observe. However, it is easily noticed because of its typical "cuckoo" call, which is heard in many areas of the countryside through the spring. Its shape and the stripes on its breast make it look like a small hawk. This resemblance often frightens small birds and drives them away from their nests. The cuckoo then lays its own single egg in the nest. Consequently, the young cuckoo is raised by a warbler, a blackcap, a reed warbler, or by a variety of other species of small insect-eating birds. The cuckoo chick develops very quickly and soon pushes the other eggs out of the nest.

Opposite page: Several typical birds of a country environment are pictured here. The birds that are not flying are shown in their preferred areas. *From left to right and from top to bottom:* cuckoo, buzzard, little owl, goldfinches, golden oriole, kestrel falcon, chaffinch, greenfinch, blackbird, shrike, nightingale, robin, and hoopoe.

Two young captive kestrel falcons feed on prey. Note the leather thongs on the legs of the bird on the right. The bird on the left is spreading its wings in order to shield the prey from the sight of rival birds.

A harvest mouse in its typical environment balances on the stem of a grass plant. The grabbing ability of the tail helps this animal in climbing the stems of plants. This seed-eating animal is 4 to 5.5 inches (11 to 14 cm) long (of which about half is made up of the tail). It weighs 0.17 to 0.31 ounces (5 to 9 g), making it the smallest rodent in Europe.

Sometimes it even pushes the other newborn birds out of the nest.

Several birds of prey, especially the common buzzard, can be found in the open and wooded countryside. This bird resembles a small hawk. Also in the countryside is the small kestrel falcon, another adaptable bird. These are the only two species of birds of prey that are able to adapt to almost all environmental changes. Generally, their populations are not declining.

Mammals of the Cultivated Steppe

Among the mammals that live in the country are many small rodents, as well as the hare, several small carnivores, and various insectivores. Ground voles and mice are the most noteworthy of the many species of rodents. The two families in which these animals belong have the largest number of species of all the mammal families.

The most common voles are meadow voles and bank voles. They eat insects, plants, and every type of seed. They reproduce rapidly and give birth to litters of eight young about every three weeks. From time to time, they multiply to

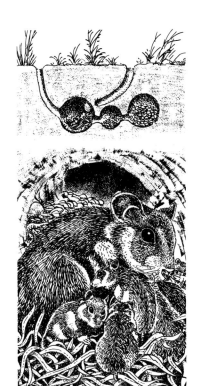

very high population levels. Densities of up to thirty thousand voles have been counted in an area of 2.5 acres (1 ha), which is equivalent to about three per square yard.

The hamster is widespread in central Europe. It is very similar to, but much larger than, the golden hamster which is often kept as a pet. Hamsters sometimes multiply to great numbers and cause great damage to cultivated crops.

The most common mouse in these environments is the species called the wood mouse or the field mouse. It resembles the closely related house mouse. The handsome harvest mouse is much smaller. Its tail can grab hold of objects, which helps it climb up the stems of grain plants. Here it builds its nest. The nest is ball-shaped and resembles the nest of a European pochard duck.

The hare is well known to European hunters. It is much larger than the wild rabbit, reaching a weight of up to 11 pounds (5 kg). The paws and ears of the hare are larger than those of the rabbit. The hare does not dig tunnels. It gives birth to the young in a den which is a simple hollow in the ground, hidden among the vegetation.

Unlike the young of rabbits, which are born blind and naked, the young of hares are born covered with hair and with their eyes open. The litters of hares, which are not as large as those of rabbits, number from one to four young. In the spring, the males fiercely fight each other for control of a mating territory. They follow one another, then face each other while standing on their hind legs. They scratch at their opponent with their front paws, tearing away large clumps of fur.

Today, because of extensive hunting of this animal, it has become necessary to repopulate the environment with hares raised in captivity. The raising of hares has become an important industry, since this animal is practically the only wild mammal of the cultivated fields of Europe that can be legally hunted.

The insectivorous mammals of the European regions include different types of shrews and the hedgehog. These animals live in cultivated areas as well as the forests. The open country is the preferred habitat of the mole, an animal species that leads an underground life.

This small mammal has strong front feet that are used in digging, and a thick, velvety black fur with bluish reflections. The mole has small eyes, and it has no outer ears. It lives almost entirely underground, digging long tunnels just a few inches below the ground surface. It feeds mainly on

From top to bottom: The illustrations show a hamster den and a female hamster with the already-weaned young in the central chamber. Hamsters are among the mammals with the highest rates of reproduction.

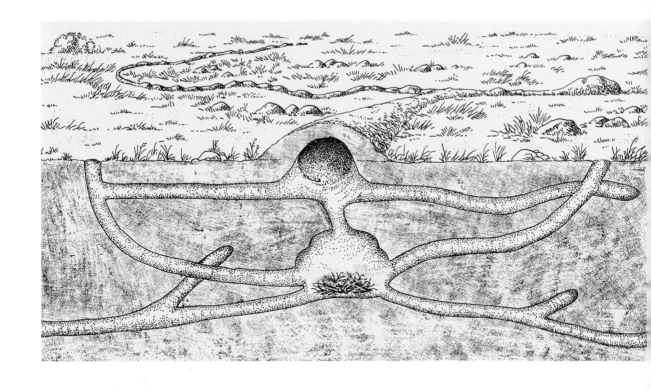

Above: Moles are known to dig intricate systems of tunnels. The shallowest tunnels (those that leave traces of soil on the surface) are dug during the reproductive period by males that search for females, which are found in the shallowest layers of the soil. Moles spend most of their time digging in the soil (top right), but when necessary they are able to swim across a small body of water (bottom right).

Right: The weasel is the smallest and most aggressive of the European carnivores. Although it does not exceed a length of 10 to 12 inches (25 to 30 cm) and a weight of 2 to 3.5 ounces (60 to 100 g), it is able to kill adult rats and small rabbits. However, it usually feeds on small rodents and lizards.

snails, but it also eats insects, reptiles, and small mice and shrews. Every day it eats an amount of food that is twice the weight of its body. Such large quantities of food are required by this animal because of the great amount of energy that is uses while digging.

From time to time, while working on its tunnels, the mole opens a vent-hole through which it pushes unwanted dirt to the surface. This gives rise to piles of dirt that are often seen in fields and gardens. It has been shown that the mole can move faster in its tunnels than a person can walk.

With this large variety of small animals, the two species of carnivores found in the cultivated zones—the weasel and the stone marten—have a large selection of prey to hunt. The roles played by these two carnivores are different since the weasel is the smallest of all the European carnivores with a length of 10 to 12 inches (25 to 30 cm), while the stone marten is about the same size as a pine marten at 22 inches (55 cm) in length. The stone marten can be distinguished from the pine marten by the yellow spot below the throat area.

Animals of the Cities

A rather large number of birds, mammals, reptiles, amphibians, and invertebrates have learned, and are learning, to live with humans in city parks, gardens, cemeteries, and in other "artificial green" environments. For example, in the cities of London and Berlin, about 120 bird species have been found to nest. Since there are so many, only a few species of birds and mammals that spend their entire lives within the center of the city will be discussed.

The house sparrow coexists with humans to a great degree. It often depends on people for food and for the construction of nests. The house sparrow builds nests between roof tiles, in holes, on telephone poles, and so forth. The adult sparrows feed mainly on plant material. While raising their young, however, they catch insects. In summer, groups of young sparrows that have just left the nest search for seeds in open fields. In the fall and winter, large flocks of sparrows also search for seeds in the open country.

The Eurasian tree sparrow is smaller than the house sparrow. It is less commonly found in cities. It is found mainly in the country, where it nests in farm buildings and trees. It is a highly social animal. Outside of the reproductive period, it gathers in flocks of hundreds of birds which often mix with house sparrows and greenfinches.

A flock of house martins roosts on telephone wires. Before migrating, these birds gather in groups that become larger and larger each day. These flocks may reach the size of one hundred or even one thousand birds before they begin their long migration. House martins resemble swallows, but they have a shorter tail, a white back, and a different call made while flying. Like swallows and swifts, house martins rely on their speed and agility to escape predators.

Street pigeons are as well known as house sparrows. The street pigeon originated from ancient domestic pigeons which returned to the wild. These ancestors continued to cross with new domestic pigeons that fled captivity. They also underwent (and still do today) a certain amount of natural selection (gradual change).

Street pigeons are quite varied, although many of them have the dark blue color of the wild rock dove. The favorable conditions offered by the city (numerous shelters, a higher temperature, artificially supplied food, and scarcity

of predators) allow these birds to reproduce much more frequently than their relatives that live on the steep rock cliffs of the seacoast.

In the city, pet cats are the main enemy of pigeons, but occasionally birds of prey also capture them. Birds of prey help to reduce the sometimes-too-large population of pigeons. The most common of these birds of prey are the kestrel falcon, the little owl, and the barn owl. When these predatory birds become adapted to eating birds, they normally raid the pigeons nests. Since the pigeons do not migrate for the winter, they are a year-round food source for these predatory birds.

The swallows and house martins have the opposite type of diet. Although they build their mud nests in the city and have little fear of humans, these birds do not depend on people for their food. They feed on flying insects and migrate to Africa for the winter.

The swifts live in much the same way as swallows and house martins. Although at first glance the swift may resemble the swallow, the two birds actually belong to separate scientific classification groups. Swifts have the same general features as swallows. Their very long wings allow them to fly high and fast. Their feet are so small that swifts cannot stand on the ground or roost on wires or other similar perching spots. When they are not flying, swifts support themselves by clinging with their claws to walls, eaves, or cliffs. They use a resting method that is similar to that of bats, with which they share the choice of holes and cracks for nesting.

The mammals that are most typically found in the city are several species of bats and mice. Bats are known for their unusual appearance as well as their ability to guide themselves in the dark. They use a system of high-frequency sound reflection that is similar to radar. In order to pick up reflected sound waves, most bats have unusual structures such as strange membranes on the lips or nose (as in the greater horseshoe bat) or enormous ears (as in the long-eared bats and other species).

Like swallows and swifts, European bats are strictly insectivorous, and they hunt only in flight. In a certain sense, at night the bats fill the role that the swallows and swifts carry out during the day. When flying insects disappear, bats hibernate instead of migrating. In spring, the females give birth to only one young. The newborn bat remains attached to the breast of the mother, even while flying.

GUIDE TO AREAS OF NATURAL INTEREST

A trip across the natural environments of central Europe is not difficult or dangerous. It can be very interesting and full of surprises. The best means of transportation is the automobile. In Europe there is a good highway system with many service stations in each of the countries.

Buying film and camera accessories is not a problem, except perhaps in several countries in the East. Here only certain brands may be available. Binoculars are very helpful in the marsh areas and in open areas such as cultivated fields, orchards, and the true steppe (which is now found in rather small areas). In the forest, however, the observation of any animal is difficult or rare. Often one must be content to note the presence of birds by their songs and calls, and the presence of mammals by their tracks.

There are different guidebooks available that are very informative and contain useful illustrations of animal tracks and other traces and signs of wary and timid animals. Also available are accurate recordings of songs and calls of all the European birds.

In any case, a good tape recorder would be a useful instrument in the forest to capture at least the loudest and most typical calls. These recorded calls can later be played back along with a commercial tape in order to identify the birds.

Rubber boots are very useful in just about any natural area. Boots allow the visitor to enter wetlands and standing water. A good rule of thumb is to wear dull-colored clothing, generally green or maroon. When planning to spend a great deal of time in one area, it is a good idea to bring along a small "blind" (such as a small tent). This makes it possible to watch animals close up without being detected by them.

If you have a strong interest in nature study and want to use the entire day, it is best to rise about an hour before dawn. To see the most wildlife, move slowly and quietly. It takes skill and patience to study wildlife.

Try to keep the sun behind you in order to best observe the colors of the animals. Some wildlife observers hide close to an animal's nest and wait for it to return.

Opposite page: A sunset unfolds on the Ticino River, which is a northern tributary of the Po River in Italy. This river is one of the most beautiful streams originating in the mountains. For several years now, it has been the center of a large park located between the Lombardy and Piedmont regions. A nature trip in central Europe is easy because of the excellent highway system and tourist services that are found practically everywhere. Although Europe is highly urbanized, there are still natural areas to be explored. These areas are well-populated by large and small animals.

FRANCE

Les Dombes (1)

This is an area of about 386 sq. miles (1,000 sq. km) of cultivated fields, forests, and ponds. The ponds cover an area of 42 sq. miles (110 sq. km) and are very important for many species of aquatic birds that nest and pause here during their migrations. Some of these birds are herons,

As shown in the map, the geographic area considered in this book excludes the mountainous areas. The list of parks does not include the British Islands and the Soviet Union, although from a biogeographic standpoint, they are rather similar to the rest of the continent. From the geographic standpoint, however, they would be included in the Atlantic region and in the northern regions.

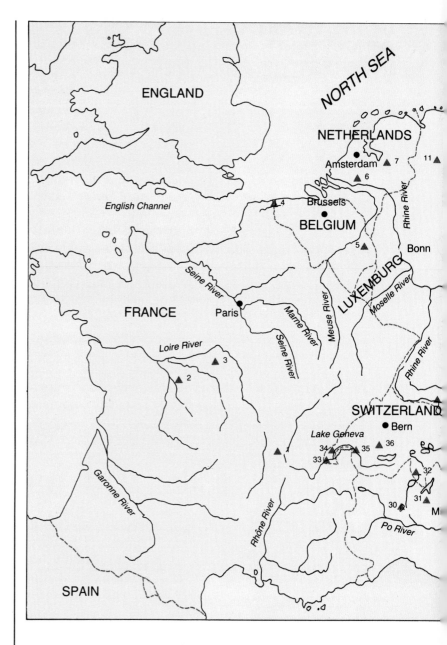

ducks, rails, coots, gallinules, and grebes.

The area is situated near the city of Lyon, from which it is easily reached.

This area covers 386 sq. miles (1,000 sq. km), enclosing about five hundred small lakes and ponds. The area is presently not protected but is very important for many species of aquatic birds. In this region are herons, bitterns,

La Brenne (2)

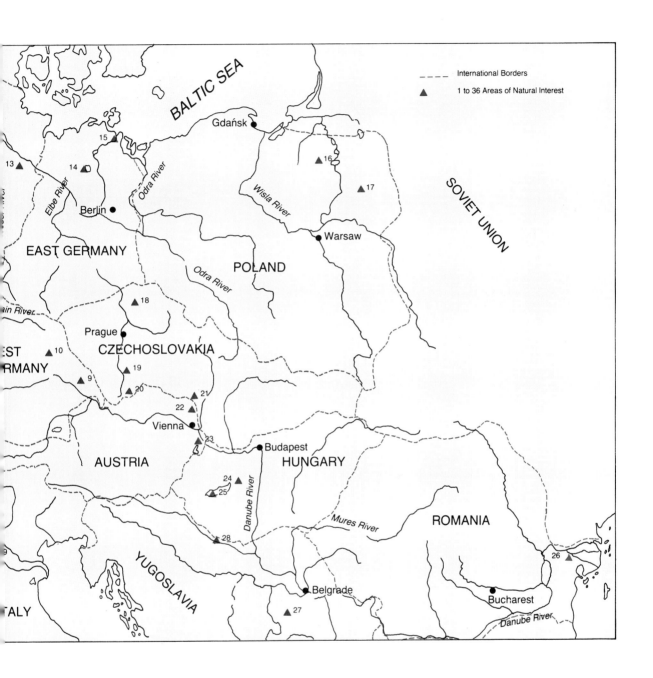

ducks, harriers (marsh hawks), rails, coots, gallinules, lapwings, and many small perching birds that are typical of marshes and open areas.

La Sologne (3)

This vast area of 1,447 sq. miles (3,750 sq. km) is very important for aquatic birds, although it is not presently protected. It is located between the Loire and the Cher rivers, less than 93 miles (150 km) south of Paris. It is easily reached from various cities such as Fert-St. Aubin, Lamotte-Beuvron, Nouan, or Salbris.

Many aquatic birds such as grebes, herons, ducks, harriers (marsh hawks), shorebirds, and short-eared owls inhabit this area.

BELGIUM

Blankaart (4)

This reserve of about 1.5 sq. miles (4 sq. km) is located southwest of the village of Woumen, on the bank of the Yser River. Little bitterns, European bitterns and harriers (marsh hawks) nest in the many reeds. In the winter, ducks and shorebirds are numerous.

Hautes Fagnes (5)

This national park of 15 sq. miles (40 sq. km) contains hills with thick forests of broadleaf trees and wetlands. There are many roe deer, European red deer, and wild boars. Curlews, buzzards, and harriers (marsh hawks) nest here, and flocks of cranes stop in the fall.

The area is located in the eastern part of Belgium, near Lige.

NETHERLANDS

Naardemeer (6)

This was the first reserve established southwest of Amsterdam in an area that is rich with ponds and marshes, surrounded by reeds. The reserve is important for the European spoonbill, a bird that does not nest in any other part of northwestern Europe. There are also red herons, cormorants, harriers (marsh hawks), tufted ducks, and reed warblers.

The reserve can only be visited by boat, and the visitor must be accompanied by authorized personnel. The headquarters can be reached by buses from Wibaustraat.

De Hoge Veluwe (7)

This national park covers an area of 21 sq. miles (56 sq. km). The St. Hubert hunting lodge and museum are located in the northern area, which is the most urbanized part. In this part of the park, cultivated fields alternate with gardens and tree farms. In the eastern part are moss-covered dunes. The central and southern parts consist of a large area of heath, meadows, birches, and conifer trees. Here and there one finds scattered oak and beech woods, reminders of the original forest. Only one road and one bicycle path cross this area which is called "Wildbaan." To the west is a large juniper nursery. The northeast area is an uncultivated wet moor with marshes and small ponds.

The park is populated by red deer, roe deer, mouflon

(wild sheep), wild boars, rabbits, hares, foxes, and squirrels. The birds include capercaillies, goshawks, wrynecks, curlews, northern shrikes, and various species of woodpeckers.

The area can be reached from the east along the roads to Arnhem and Apeldoorn, and from the west along the road to Ede.

WEST GERMANY

Costance (8)

The shores of Lake Constance, near the borders of West Germany, Switzerland, and Austria, are mainly wet environments. Eight species of ducks nest here, and 100,000 to 200,000 ducks and coots winter in this area, along with many shorebirds. There are also rare and interesting plants and many amphibians and insects. At Mettnau, near Radolfzell, there is a famous bird observatory.

Bayerischer Wald (9)

This national park extends over an area of about 46 sq. miles (120 sq. km) east of Regensburg, between the Danube River and the border with Czechoslovakia. Most of the park is covered by forests of white spruce, Norway spruce, and beech. The animals include red deer, roe deer, buzzards, honey buzzards, goshawks, sparrow hawks, capercaillies, large-headed little owls, and various species of woodpeckers and perching birds.

Pfalzer Wald (10)

This area covers about 64 sq. miles (167 sq. km), and it is the most thickly wooded territory of West Germany. It is composed primarily of conifer trees, mixed with beech and oak trees. This large area of forest is interrupted only along the Weinstrasse, where vineyards are located. The animals found here include red deer, roe deer, wild boars, many small mammals, and more than two hundred species of birds. Near Wachenheim, in the Wildschutzpark Kurpfalz, there are wisents (European bison), mouflon (wild sheep), and wild goats inside fenced areas.

Diepholzer Morniederung (11)

This marshy area, covering about 69 sq. miles (180 sq. km), is located 23 miles (37 km) southwest of Osnabruck. Many species of locally rare aquatic birds nest here, such as the golden plover pairs, the greater curlew, the European teal, and a certain species of sandpiper.

Dummer (12)

This natural park contains the last remains of a large marshy area located near Niedersachsen, 40 miles (65 km) southwest of Bremen. Its original 154 sq. miles (400 sq. km)

This photo shows a broad-leaved forest in the Voges Mountains (France). The remaining primary or secondary forest in Europe is rather small in total area of forest cover, but the number of European species threatened by extinction is lower in respect to those of any other continent.

have been reduced to the present 14 sq. miles (36 sq. km). Still, various species of rather rare aquatic birds either nest here or come to this area to spend the winter.

Covering an area of 77 sq. miles (200 sq. km), this national park was set up at the beginning of this century with the aim of protecting the natural life of this area. Existing buildings were made part of the park, an example being the restoration of old farms built in traditional styles. The landscape has rounded hills covered by heath and conifer forests. The mammals here include red deer, roe deer, foxes, pine martens, and squirrels. The 120 species of birds include black grouse, goshawks, hobbies, kestrel falcons, black woodpeckers, curlews, and snipes.

Luneberg (13)

This is the largest lake in East Germany, covering an area of 451 sq. miles (1,170 sq. km). It is important for studies of birds and bodies of water. The mute swan, greylag goose, and many species of ducks nest here. Many cranes stop here in the fall.

The area is located just south of Warem, in the district of Neubrandenburg.

EAST GERMANY

Muritz (14)

These are two lakes that formed in a basin that developed following the retreat of the Quaternary glaciers.

The water is shallow and eutrophic (with a high content of nutrients and a low oxygen level). Part of the total area of 46 sq. miles (120 sq. km) is included in natural reserves. These reserves are an important refuge for rare plants such as bird's-eye primrose and birds such as the mute swan. The lakes also are used for raising carp.

The area is located south of Anklam, at the spring of the Landgraben and Zarrow rivers.

Putzarer and Galenbecker (15)

POLAND

Mazuri and Augustow (16)

The district of these two lakes lies between the Russian border and the Baltic Sea. This is a very beautiful area, rich with forests and lakes that are a true paradise for aquatic birds. Among the many species are red-necked grebes and little grebes, black storks, white storks, greylag geese, cranes, black kites, goshawks, harriers (marsh hawks), peregrine falcons, coralline gulls, and occasionally, greater terns.

The district contains four small reserves. Kudypy Reserve, which is 13 sq. miles (34.5 sq. km), is located along the Pasleka River. It was set up in 1958 to protect a beaver colony. The vegetation is composed of mixed forests of broadleaf trees and pines. Czerwone Reserve covers 8 sq. miles (21 sq. km) and has forests with moors, where groups of moose freely graze.

Marycha Reserve covers 0.7 sq. miles (1.9 sq. km) and lies near Sejny in the Wigry Forest, which is mainly composed of pines, birches, poplars, and alders. These trees provide construction materials for the many beavers that live along the Czarna River.

Osiedle Kormoranow Reserve covers 12 acres (5 ha) and is located within the Rzecznica Forest, near Czluchov. This is an old forest of beech trees along the banks of the Brda River. It is inhabited by the largest colony of cormorants in Poland, with over 150 nests.

Bialowieza (17)

This national park of 196 sq. miles (507 sq. km) is composed of a large virgin forest, covering a plain. Marshy zones alternate with patches of forest that include pines, Norway spruce, hornbeams, and a large variety of shrubs that make up the thick underbrush. The animal population is extremely interesting, including mammals such as wisents (European bison), moose, lynx, and brown bears. The birds include eagle owls, long-eared owls, white storks, black storks, two species of eagles, three-toed woodpeckers, white-backed woodpeckers, capercaillies, kites, red-breasted flycatchers, and hoopoes.

Only guided tours of the park are permitted.

CZECHOSLOVAKIA

Novozamecky Rybnik (18)

This reserve of 1.3 sq. miles (3.5 sq. km) is located about 28 miles (45 km) north of Prague, near Ceska Lipa. It includes one of the oldest artificial fishing lakes, dug in the thirteenth century in the valley of a tributary of the Plouc-nice River. The vegetation consists of shore forests of alder and willow, as well as vast reed beds and areas of water lilies. The animals include otters, herons, greylag geese, ducks, black kites, harriers (marsh hawks), ospreys, kingfishers, and perching birds typical of marshes.

Maly a Velky Tisy (19)

This reserve of 2 sq. miles (6.1 sq. km) is located north of Ceske Budejovice and Trebon, not far from the reserve of Stara Reka. It includes a system of different artificial fishing lakes, dug about five hundred years ago and connected to the Zlata Stoka golden canal. The shore forest has alders, willows, oaks, and basswoods. The marsh vegetation consists of reeds, wild calla, marsh orchids, water lilies, and other plants. The animals include many birds such as herons, night herons, bitterns, ducks, grebes, shorebirds, terns, and small perching birds typical of marshes. There also are many fish.

The reserve is normally closed to the public, except for scientific study.

Stara Reka (20)

Extending over an area of 5 sq. miles (12 sq. km) along a section of a large tributary of the Luznice River, this reserve includes many canals, ponds, and artificial lakes. A typical riverbank forest is found here, consisting of willows, alders, beech, maples, and oaks. Reeds, white and yellow water lilies, and swimming water-nut plants grow in the water. The most interesting animal found here is the otter.

The reserve is located between Trebon and the Austrian border, 15 miles (25 km) east of Ceske Budejovice.

Lednicke Ribniki (21)

This reserve of 2.1 sq. miles (5.5 sq. km) includes four old artificial fishing lakes which surround the castle of Ladnice, as well as several meadows and adjacent woods. The vegetation near the shore consists of alders, willows, oaks, reed-grasses, cattails, and irises, as well as small salt-water areas with slender glasswort plants. There are at least 130 species of birds that nest here, including grebes, cormorants, herons, bitterns, black storks, greylag geese, avocets, and many species of ducks and perching birds.

The reserve is located in the extreme southeastern part of Czechoslovakia, just west of Breclav. The public can enter the park by special trails.

There are many other interesting wetland areas in Czechoslovakia, among which are the ponds of Docsy at 4 sq. miles (10 sq. km), and the Trebon basin, which is an important area for migrating waterfowl, covering 231 sq. miles (600 sq. km).

AUSTRIA

Marchausen (22)

This nature reserve covers 4 sq. miles (11 sq. km) and follows the western bank of the March River at the border with Czechoslovakia. The reserve includes one of the largest and most beautiful watersheds of Europe, with a rich vegetation consisting of reeds, willows, poplars, elderberry shrubs, oaks, and elms. The animals include red deer, roe deer, wild boars, hares, martens, otters, and occasionally lynxes. However, birds are the major attraction. This area has the last Austrian colonies of cormorants and night herons, as well as various species of woodpeckers, owls, cranes, curlews, teals, black storks, eagles, falcons, and goshawks.

Originally the land was privately owned by an aristocratic family, and it surrounds the castle where the family lived. Today, the castle serves as the headquarters for the management of the reserve, and it also contains a hunting museum.

Neusiedl and Seewinkel (23)

Neusiedl Lake is a large, shallow lake located in the steppe. The area of Seewinkel, near the border with Hungary, is a marshy region with many ponds and small saltwater lakes. The total areas add up to 132 sq. miles (341 sq. km). These environments are ideal for the nesting of numerous waterfowl, in particular herons, grebes, mallards, and other ducks, rails, corn crakes, geese, bitterns, and storks.

There is an important bird study station at Illmitz, on the shore of Lake Neusiedl.

HUNGARY

Velence (24)

Lake Velence covers an area of 10 sq. miles (26 sq. km) about 28 miles (45 km) southwest of Budapest. It is especially important for the nesting of the great egret and for the wintering of geese, numbering up to twenty thousand birds.

Balaton and Kisbalaton (25)

Lake Balaton covers an area of 212 sq. miles (550 sq. km), making it the largest lake of Hungary and one of the largest European lakes. This lake is of natural importance because up to forty-thousand geese winter here.

The Kisbalaton Marsh is separated from Lake Balaton by flood plain deposits. This marsh of 16 sq. miles (42 sq. km) has a rich growth of reeds. It is important for the nesting of cormorants, night herons, squacco herons, snowy egrets, great egrets, spoonbills, and many ducks. A research station has been established in this area.

ROMANIA

Delta of the Danube River (26)

The delta of the Danube River is one of the most fascinating and productive environments of Europe. The structure of the marshes, lagoons, lakes, and minor tributaries is the result of the effect of the Danube River, the Black Sea, the rich vegetation and in modern times, humans. About 159 sq. miles (412 sq. km) are organized into natural reserves where

A boat travels through the marsh of Kopacki Rit in Yugoslavia. European wetlands have been greatly reduced in size during the last century. Those that have been preserved, however, are carefully protected.

hunting is strictly prohibited. Fishing is permitted only in the summer to a certain number of people. The reed beds are burned occasionally under the strict supervision of biologists.

Among the animals that live in the reeds are wild boars, otters, minks, foxes, wildcats, and nutrias. The land turtles, which are now rare along the coasts of the Black Sea, are very common near Lakes Razelm and Sfintu Gheorghe. The delta is truly a paradise for birds. This area is crossed by five different migration routes. Many northern species spend the winter here, while others nest here during the summer. The rarer species include pelicans, spoonbills, great egrets, small cormorants, and cranes. The waterfowl that spend the winter here include four species of geese, swans, loons, and many species of ducks.

The three reserves protect the three most important types of habitat: the lagoon, the coastal delta, and the interior lands. Rosca-Buhariova-Hrecisca is located in the area north of the delta. It is formed by marshes crossed by an extensive network of small streams. It is inhabited by a large European colony of pelicans. Owls live in the oak woods along the banks of the Letea River. Large nests of the sea eagle can be easily spotted. Some of the mammals found here are mink, otters, ermine, nutria, and foxes. Perisor-Zatoane covers 54 sq. miles (140 sq. km) and includes the oldest zone of the delta, south of the arm of Sfintu Gheorghe Lake. Its coastal margin contains long, recently formed parallel banks of sand and isolated lakes. Where the river meets the sea, fresh water mixes with the salt water, creating a marshy environment that is ideal for the nesting of swans, the great egrets, red herons, and snowy egrets. Peritesca-Leahove is a zone of dry sandbanks and shallow lagoons west of the Perisor Reserve. Like the Perisor Reserve, it represents an ideal environment for the nesting of coastal birds. It also is ideal for the wintering of species that are adapted to the variations of salinity (saltiness) of the inner lagoons and marshes.

YUGOSLAVIA

Obedska Bara (27)

This well-known marsh area covers 67 sq. miles (175 sq. km) southwest of Belgrade. Of this, 4 sq. miles (10 sq. km) are nature reserve. Among the birds that nest there are bitterns, night herons, white and black storks, snowy egrets, red herons, glossy ibises, spoonbills, and many other aquatic birds.

Kopacki Rit (28)

This reserve of 68 sq. miles (177 sq. km) is another beautiful marshy area in Yugoslavia, found between the Drava and the Danube rivers about 10 miles (16 km) northeast of Osijek (Croatia). A little over one-third of the area is flooded. Cormorants, snowy egrets, great egrets, white storks, geese, and sea eagles nest in this area. Flocks of migrating cranes arrive in late autumn.

ITALY

Fontana Forest (29)

This area of only 568 acres (2.3 sq. km) is located just north of Mantova. It is one of the best examples of a plains forest in the Po River valley, having survived the extensive cutting of forests for agricultural reasons. Many woodpeckers and black kites nest here, as well as other birds.

Groane (31)

This park includes a total area of 386 sq. miles (1,000 sq. km) found along the Ticino River, from Sesto Calende to Pavia and beyond. This park protects large areas of forest environment and various animals, including wild boars, nesting colonies of herons and bitterns, ducks, lapwings, and snipes.

Ticino (30)

This park of about 11 sq. miles (30 sq. km) is located northeast of Milan and is reached from the road that leads from Monza to Saronno. About one-fifth of the park is composed of British oak, Scotch pine trees, and moors. It is inhabited by numerous forest birds.

SWITZERLAND

Magadino (32)

The delta of the Ticino and Verzasca rivers, emptying into Lake Maggiore at Magadino (near Lucerne), is one of the most beautiful wetland areas of the Ticino Canton. The area contains a rich marsh vegetation and many nesting aquatic birds. Migrating birds also stop here in the winter.

Delta of the Rhone River (33)

From Noville, people can drive to Les Grangettes from which the Grand Canal is only a fifteen-minute walk away. Other interesting areas are the Vieux Rhone, the ponds of Muraz and Chaux-Rossa, and the shore of Lake Lemano, on the right side of the river. Many coots, great crested grebes, ducks, black kites, and other birds make their homes in this area.

Haute Versoix (34)

This marsh is reached from Chavanne (north of Geneva). It is a long strip of wetland area along both riverbanks,

which marks the border between Switzerland and France. Many birds nest among the thick aquatic vegetation. These include curlews and harriers (marsh hawks). There are otters and a small colony of beavers, which were released into this area by a nature conservation association of Geneva.

Neuchatel (35)

This lake is 1,640 feet (500 m) wide and about 24 miles (40 km) long, and is one of the most interesting lakes of Switzerland. A large number of aquatic birds nest in its large reed beds. These include great crested grebes (200 pairs), common terns (180 pairs), several mergansers, and many gulls. Wild geese, grebes, and cormorants winter here.

The most interesting area is located on the eastern part of the lake, between Cudrefin and Zihl Canal. From Cudrefin, visitors can easily walk or bicycle down the trail that skirts the marsh.

Aare (36)

Exiting from the Bern-Thun highway at Rubigen, visitors can leave the car in the nearby locality of Campagna and walk among the thick forests that border the Aare River between Bern and Thul (there are several well-marked trails). This area of river wetlands and marshy woods is one of the most typical areas of Switzerland and all of central Europe.

GLOSSARY

abundant very plentiful; more than enough.

adaptation change or adjustment by which a species or individual improves its condition in relationship to its environment.

algae primitive organisms which resemble plants but do not have true roots, stems, or leaves. Algae are usually found in water or damp places.

basin all the land drained by a river and its branches.

bog wet, spongy ground; a small marsh or swamp. There are many peat bogs in central Europe.

camouflage a disguise or concealment of any kind.

conifers cone-bearing trees and shrubs, most of which are evergreens.

conservation the controlled use and systematic protection of natural resources, such as forests and waterways.

continent one of the principal land masses of the earth. Africa, Antarctica, Asia, Europe, North America, South America, and Australia are regarded as continents.

cultivated to prepare and use soil or land for growing crops.

deciduous trees trees that shed their leaves at a specific season or stage of growth.

den the cave or other home of a wild animal.

diurnal active during the day.

domesticate to tame wild animals and breed them for many purposes.

dormant alive, but not actively growing; in a state of suspended animation.

ecology the relationship between organisms and their environment. The science and study of ecology is extremely important as a means of preserving all the forms of life on earth.

environment the circumstances or conditions of a plant or animal's surroundings.

extinction the process of destroying or extinguishing. Many species of plant and animal life face extinction either because of natural changes in the environment or those caused by the carelessness of people.

fossil a remnant or trace of an organism of a past geologic age, such as a skeleton or leaf imprint, embedded in some part of the earth's crust.

germinate to sprout or cause to sprout or grow.

glaciers gigantic moving sheets of ice that covered great areas of the earth in an earlier time. Glaciers existed primarily in the Pleistocene epoch, one million years ago.

habitat the areas or type of environment in which a person or other organism normally occurs.

herbivore an animal that eats plants.

hibernate to spend the winter in a dormant state.

impermeable not permitting fluids to pass through; impenetrable. Impermeable land remains wet after rain.

insectivore an animal that eats insects.

invertebrate lacking a backbone or spinal column.

lagoon a shallow body of water, especially one separated from the sea by sandbars or coral reefs.

larva the early, immature form of any animal that changes structurally when it becomes an adult. This process of change is called metamorphosis.

legume any of a large family of herbs, shrubs, and trees, including peas, beans, and clover.

lichen a primitive plant formed by the association of blue-green algae with fungi.

litter the young born at one time by an animal which normally bears several young at one delivery.

marsh an area of low-lying flatland, such as a swamp or bog. The marsh is a type of borderland between dry ground and water.

meteorologist a scientist who studies the atmosphere and the earth's weather.

migrate to move from one region to another with the change in seasons.

moor a tract of open, rolling wasteland, usually covered with heather and often marshy or peaty.

naturalist a person who studies nature, especially by direct observation of animals and plants.

niche the specific space occupied by an organism within its habitat; a small space or hollow.

nocturnal referring to animals that are active at night.

observatory a building equipped for scientific observation or study, especially one having a huge telescope for astronomical research.

omnivorous an animal that eats both plants and other animals.

peat a partly decayed, moisture-absorbing plant matter found in ancient bogs and swamps, used as a plant covering or fuel.

photosynthesis the process by which chlorophyll-containing cells in green plants convert sunlight into chemical energy and change inorganic compounds into organic compounds.

plumage the feathers of a bird. A bird's plumage can provide camouflage, aid in identification, and play an important role in mating rituals.

pollute to make unclean, impure; to contaminate. The delicate balance of nature is often disturbed by pollution.

predator an animal that lives by preying on others.

prey an animal hunted or killed for food by another.

quills the prickly spines of a porcupine or hedgehog, used as weapons for defense.

refuge shelter or protection from danger or difficulty; a place of safety.

reptile a cold-blooded vertebrate having lungs, a bony skeleton, and a body covered with scales or horny plates.

scavenger any animal that eats refuse (garbage) and decaying organic matter.

species a distinct kind, sort, variety, or class. Plant and animal species have a high degree of similarity and can generally interbreed only among themselves.

steppe a large plain having few trees. Many of the steppes in central Europe have been cultivated and planted with graincrops.

terrestrial living on land rather than in water, the sky, or trees.

tributary a small stream which flows into another, larger one.

tundra a treeless area between the ice cap and the tree line of arctic regions, having a permanently frozen subsoil.

vegetarian a person or animal that eats no meat and sometimes no animal products.

vertebrate having a backbone or spinal column.

INDEX